ON SUCCESS
Charles T. Munger

*"In your own life, what you want to maximize
is a seamless web of deserved trust."*

This reprint includes abridged materials from:
Poor Charlie's Almanack
—Expanded Third Edition—
The Wit and Wisdom of Charles T. Munger
ISBN -13 978-1-57864-501-5

For information write:

The Donning Company Publishers
184 Business Park Drive, Suite 206
Virginia Beach, VA 23462

Library of Congress
Cataloging-in-Publication Data

Munger, Charles T., 1924-
On success / Charles T. Munger. p. cm.

ISBN 978-1-57864-598-5
1. Success. 2. Success in business.
3. Decision making. I. Title.
BF637.S8M786 2009
650.1--dc22
2009037964

Printed in the United States of America
by Walsworth Publishing Company
Marceline, Missouri

This reprint was furnished to you by
Davis Advisors

Davis Distributors, LLC,
2949 East Elvira Road,
Suite 101, Tucson, AZ 85756

Compliments of

ON SUCCESS
Table of Contents

FOREWORD

I t is often said that life should come with instructions. After all, the question, "how ought one to live?" has occupied humanity since Socrates. The three talks in this volume represent Charlie Munger's answer to that ancient question. Although not as well-known as his world-famous colleague, Charlie has served as Warren Buffett's partner in running Berkshire Hathaway for more than 45 years and, in Warren's own words, is "both smarter and wiser." Clearly this is a man worth listening to.

Almost 20 years ago, a mutual friend invited me to have breakfast with Charlie. As I sat down, I hoped I would learn something about investing. When I stood up three hours later, I had not only learned invaluable lessons about investing, but also about business, psychology, history, science, human nature, and indeed life. On that day, I enrolled in what might be called the Charles T. Munger School of Remedial Worldly Wisdom—a school with no graduation date. Indeed, one of its fundamental tenets is that the quest to think clearly, behave rationally and earn trust is lifelong.

The core principles outlined in these pages sound deceptively simple: the surest way to get what you want is to deserve what you want; deliver to the world what you would buy if you were on the other end; seek out the big ideas in all disciplines and apply them to your decision making; avoid twaddle; and more. But these lessons and the examples used to illustrate them are profound, correct and enormously effective.

In short, you now hold in your hands the closest thing I have ever found to an instruction book for living a successful life. It is required reading in our family and at our firm. We send it with our best wishes and sincere thanks for your continued trust.

—Christopher C. Davis

1

HARVARD SCHOOL
COMMENCEMENT SPEECH
June 13, 1986

N ow that Headmaster Berrisford has selected one of the oldest and longest-serving trustees to make a commencement speech, it behooves the speaker to address two questions in every mind:

1) Why was such a selection made?

2) How long is the speech going to last?

I will answer the first question from long experience alongside Berrisford. He is seeking enhanced reputation for our school in the manner of the man who proudly displays his horse that can count to seven. The man knows that counting to seven is not much of a mathematical feat, but he expects approval because doing so is creditable, considering the performer is a horse.

The second question, regarding the length of the speech, I am not going to answer in advance. It would deprive your upturned faces of lively curiosity and obvious keen anticipation, which I prefer to retain, regardless of source.

But I will tell you how my consideration of speech length created the subject matter of the speech itself. I was puffed up when invited to speak. While not having significant public-speaking experience, I do hold a black belt in chutzpah, and I immediately considered Demosthenes and Cicero as role models and anticipated trying to earn a compliment like Cicero gave when asked which was his favorite among the orations of Demosthenes.

Cicero replied:

"The longest one."

However, fortunately for this audience, I also thought of Samuel Johnson's famous comment when he addressed Milton's poem "Paradise Lost" and correctly said, "No one ever wished it longer." And that made me consider which of all the twenty Harvard School graduation speeches I had heard that I had wished longer. There was only one such speech, given by Johnny Carson, specifying Carson's prescriptions for guaranteed misery in life. I, therefore, decided to repeat Carson's speech but in expanded form with some added prescriptions of my own. After all, I am much older than Carson was when he spoke and have failed and been miserable more often and in more ways than was possible for a charming humorist speaking at a younger age. I am plainly well qualified to expand on Carson's theme.

What Carson said was that he couldn't tell the graduating class how to be happy, but he could tell them from personal experience how to guarantee misery. Carson's prescription for sure misery included:

1. Ingesting chemicals in an effort to alter mood or perception;
2. Envy; and
3. Resentment.

I can still recall Carson's absolute conviction as he told how he had tried these things on occasion after occasion and had become miserable every time.

It is easy to understand Carson's first prescription for misery—ingesting chemicals. I add my voice. The four closest friends of my youth were highly intelligent, ethical, humorous types, favored in person and background. Two are long dead, with alcohol a contributing factor, and a third is a living alcoholic—if you call that living.

While susceptibility varies, addiction can happen to any of us through a subtle process where the bonds of degradation are too light to be felt until they are too strong to be broken. And yet, I have yet to meet anyone, in over six decades of life, whose life was worsened by fear and avoidance of such a deceptive pathway to destruction.

Envy, of course, joins chemicals in winning some sort of quantity prize for causing misery. It was wreaking havoc long before it got a bad press in the laws of Moses. If you wish to retain the contribution of envy to misery, I recommend that you never read any of the biographies of that good Christian, Samuel Johnson, because his life demonstrates in an enticing way the possibility and advantage of transcending envy.

Resentment has always worked for me exactly as it worked for Carson. I cannot recommend it highly enough to you if you desire misery. Johnson spoke well when he said that life is hard enough to swallow without squeezing in the bitter rind of resentment.

For those of you who want misery, I also recommend refraining from practice of the Disraeli compromise, designed for people who find it impossible to quit resentment cold turkey. Disraeli, as he rose to become one of the greatest prime ministers, learned to give up vengeance as a motivation for action, but he did retain some outlet for resentment by putting the names of people who wronged him on pieces of paper in a drawer. Then, from time to time, he reviewed these names and took pleasure in noting the way the world had taken his enemies down without his assistance.

Well, so much for Carson's three prescriptions. Here are four more prescriptions from Munger:

First, be unreliable. Do not faithfully do what you have engaged to do. If you will only master this one habit, you will more than counterbalance the combined effect of all your virtues, howsoever great. If you like being distrusted and excluded from the best human contribution and company, this prescription is for you. Master this one habit, and you will always play the role of the hare in the fable, except that instead of being outrun by one fine turtle, you will be outrun by hordes and hordes of mediocre turtles and even some mediocre turtles on crutches.

I must warn you that if you don't follow my first prescription, it may be hard to end up miserable even if you start disadvantaged. I had a roommate in college who was and is severely dyslexic. But he is perhaps the most reliable man I have ever known. He has had a wonderful life so far, outstanding wife and children, chief executive of a multibillion dollar corporation. If you want to avoid a conventional, main-culture, establishment result of this kind, you simply can't count on your other handicaps to hold you back if you persist in being reliable.

I cannot here pass by a reference to a life described as "wonderful so far," without reinforcing the "so far" aspects of the human condition by repeating the remark of Croesus, once the richest king in the world. Later, in ignominious captivity, as he prepared to be burned alive, he said: "Well now do I remember the words of the historian Solon: 'No man's life should be accounted a happy one until it is over.'"

My second prescription for misery is to learn everything you possibly can from your own experience, minimizing what you learn vicariously from the good and bad experience of others, living and dead. This prescription is a sure-shot producer of misery and second-rate achievement.

You can see the results of not learning from others' mistakes by simply looking about you. How little originality there is in the common disasters of mankind—drunk driving deaths, reckless driving maimings, incurable venereal diseases, conversion of bright college students into brainwashed zombies as members of destructive cults, business failures through repetition of obvious mistakes made by predecessors, various forms of crowd folly, and so on. I recommend as a memory clue to finding the way to real trouble from heedless, unoriginal error the modern saying: "If at first you don't succeed, well, so much for hang gliding."

The other aspect of avoiding vicarious wisdom is the rule for not learning from the best work done before yours. The prescription is to become as non-educated as you reasonably can. Perhaps you will better see the type of nonmiserable result you can thus avoid if I render a short historical account. There once was a man who assiduously mastered the work of his best predecessors, despite a poor start and very tough time in analytical geometry. Eventually, his own work attracted wide attention, and he said of his work:

"If I have seen a little farther than other men, it is because I stood on the shoulders of giants."

The bones of that man lie buried now, in Westminster Abbey, under an unusual inscription:

"Here lie the remains of all that was mortal in Sir Isaac Newton."

My third prescription to you for misery is to go down and stay down when you get your first, second, or third severe reverse in the battle of life. Because there is so much adversity out there, even for the lucky and wise, this will guarantee that, in due course, you will be permanently mired in misery. Ignore at all cost the lesson contained in the accurate epitaph written for himself by Epictetus: "Here lies Epictetus, a slave, maimed in body, the ultimate in poverty, and favored by the gods."

My final prescription to you for a life of fuzzy thinking and infelicity is to ignore a story they told me when I was very young about a rustic who said, "I wish I knew where I was going to die, and then I'd never go there." Most people smile (as you did) at the rustic's ignorance and ignore his basic wisdom. If my experience is any guide, the rustic's approach is to be avoided at all cost by someone bent on misery. To help fail, you should discount as mere quirk, with no useful message, the method of the rustic, which is the same one used in Carson's speech.

What Carson did was to approach the study of how to create X by turning the question backward, that is, by studying how to create non-X. The great algebraist, Jacobi, had exactly the same approach as Carson and was known for his constant repetition of one phrase: "Invert, always invert." It is in the nature of things, as Jacobi knew, that many hard problems are best solved only when they are addressed backward. For instance, when almost everyone else was trying to revise the electromagnetic laws of Maxwell to be consistent with the motion laws of Newton, Einstein discovered special relativity as he made a 180-degree turn and revised Newton's laws to fit Maxwell's.

It is my opinion, as a certified biography nut, that Charles Robert Darwin would have ranked near the middle of the Harvard School graduating class of 1986. Yet he is now famous in the history of science. This is precisely the type of example you should learn nothing from if bent on minimizing your results from your own endowment.

Darwin's result was due in large measure to his working method, which violated all my rules for misery and particularly emphasized a backward twist in that he always gave priority attention to evidence tending to disconfirm whatever cherished and hard-won theory he already had. In contrast, most people early achieve and later intensify a tendency to process new and disconfirming information so that any original conclusion remains intact. They become people of whom Philip Wylie observed: "You couldn't squeeze a dime between what they already know and what they will never learn."

The life of Darwin demonstrates how a turtle may outrun a hare, aided by extreme objectivity, which helps the objective person end up like the only player without a blindfold in a game of Pin the Tail on the Donkey.

If you minimize objectivity, you ignore not only a lesson from Darwin but also one from Einstein. Einstein said that his successful theories came from "Curiosity, concentration, perseverance, and self-criticism." And by self-criticism, he meant the testing and destruction of his own well-loved ideas.

Finally, minimizing objectivity will help you lessen the compromises and burden of owning worldly goods because objectivity does not work only for great physicists and biologists. It also adds power to the work of a plumbing contractor in Bemidji.

Therefore, if you interpret being true to yourself as requiring that you retain every notion of your youth, you will be safely underway, not only toward maximizing ignorance, but also toward whatever misery can be obtained through unpleasant experiences in business.

It is fitting that a backward sort of speech end with a backward sort of toast, inspired by Elihu Root's repeated accounts of how the dog went to Dover, "leg over leg." To the class of 1986:

Gentlemen, may each of you rise by spending each day of a long life aiming low.

2

USC GOULD SCHOOL OF LAW COMMENCEMENT ADDRESS

The University of Southern California
May 13, 2007

Well, no doubt many of you are wondering why this speaker is so old. (Audience laughs.) Well, the answer is obvious: He hasn't died yet. (Audience laughs.) And why was this speaker chosen? Well, I don't know that. I'd like to think that the development department had nothing to do with it.

Whatever the reason, I think it's fitting that I'm speaking here because I see a crowd of older people in the rear, not wearing robes. And I know, from having educated an army of descendants, who it is that really deserves a lot of the honors that are being given today to the robe-wearing students in front. The sacrifices, and the wisdom, and the value transfer, that come from one generation to the next should always be appreciated. I also take pleasure from the sea of Asian faces to my left. All my life I have admired Confucius. I like the idea of "filial piety," of ideas or values that are taught and duties that come naturally, that should be passed onto the next generation. You people who don't think there's anything in this idea, please note how fast Asian people are rising in American life. I think they have something.

All right, I've scratched out a few notes, and I'm going to try and give an account of certain ideas and attitudes that have worked well for me. I don't claim that they're perfect for everybody. But I think many of them contain universal values and that many of them are "can't fail" ideas.

What are the core ideas that helped me? Well, luckily I had the idea at a very early age that the safest way to try to get what you want is to try to deserve what you want. It's such a simple idea. It's the golden rule. You want to deliver to the world what you would buy if you were on the other end. There is no ethos in my opinion that is better for any lawyer or any other person to have. By and large, the people who've had this ethos win in life, and they don't win just money and honors. They win the respect, the deserved trust of the people they deal with. And there is huge pleasure in life to be obtained from getting deserved trust.

Now, occasionally, you will find a perfect rogue of a person who dies rich and widely known. But mostly these people are fully understood as despicable by the surrounding civilization. If the Cathedral is full of people at the funeral ceremony, most of them are there to celebrate the fact that the person is dead. That reminds me of the story of the time when one of these people died, and the Minister said, "It's now time to say something nice about the deceased." And nobody came forward, and nobody came forward, and nobody came forward. And finally one man came up and said, "Well, his brother was worse." (Audience laughs.) That is not where you want to go. A life ending in such a funeral is not the life you want to have.

The second idea that I developed very early is that there's no love that's so right as admiration-based love, and such love should include the instructive dead. Somehow I picked up that idea, and I've lived with it all my life. It's been very useful to me. A love like that described by Somerset Maugham in his book, *Of Human Bondage*, is a sick kind of love. It's a disease, and if you find yourself with a disease like that, you should eliminate it.

Another idea, and this may remind you of Confucius, too, is that the acquisition of wisdom is a moral duty. It's not something you do just to advance in life. And there's a corollary to that idea that is very important. It requires that you're hooked on lifetime learning. Without lifetime learning, you people are not going to do very well. You are not going to get very far in life based on what you already know. You're going to advance in life by what you learn after you leave here.

Consider Berkshire Hathaway, one of the best-regarded corporations in the world. It may have the best long-term, big-assets-involving investment record in the history of civilization. The skill that got Berkshire through one decade would not have sufficed to get it through the next decade, with comparable levels of achievement. Warren Buffett had to be a continuous-learning machine. The same requirement exists in lower walks of life. I constantly see people rise in life who are not the smartest, sometimes not even the most diligent. But they are learning machines. They go to bed every night a little wiser than they were that morning. And boy, does that habit help, particularly when you have a long run ahead of you.

Alfred North Whitehead correctly said at one time that the rapid advance of civilization came only when man "invented the method of invention." He was referring to the huge growth in GDP per capita and many other good things we now take for granted. Big-time progress started a few hundred years ago. Before that progress per century was almost nil. Just as civilization can progress only when it invents the method of invention, you can progress only when you learn the method of learning.

I was very lucky. I came to law school having learned the method of learning, and nothing has served me better in my long life than continuous learning. Consider Warren Buffett again. If you watched him with a time clock, you'd find that about half of his waking time is spent reading. Then a big chunk of the rest of his time is spent talking one-on-one, either on the telephone or personally, with highly gifted people whom he trusts and who trust him. Viewed up close, Warren looks quite academic as he achieves worldly success.

Academia has many wonderful values in it. I came across an example not too long ago. In my capacity as a hospital board chairman, I was dealing with a medical school academic named Joseph M. Mirra, M.D. This man, over years of disciplined work, made himself know more about bone tumor pathology than almost anyone else in the world. He wanted to pass this knowledge on to help treat bone cancer. How was he going to do it? Well, he decided to write a textbook, and even though I don't think a textbook like this sells more than a few thousand copies, they do end up in cancer treatment centers all over the world. He took a sabbatical year and sat down at his computer with all his slides, carefully saved and organized. He worked seventeen hours a day, seven days a week, for a year. Some sabbatical. At the end of the year he had created one of the two great bone tumor pathology textbooks of the world. When you're around values like Mirra's, you want to pick up as much as you can.

Another idea that was hugely useful to me was one I obtained when I listened in law school when some waggish professor said, "A legal mind is a mind that considers it feasible and useful, when two things are all twisted up together and interacting, to try to think about one thing without considering the other." Well, I could see from that indirectly pejorative sentence that any such "legal" approach was ridiculous. And this pushed me further along in my natural drift, which was toward learning all the big ideas in all the big disciplines, so I wouldn't be the perfect damn fool the professor described. And because the really big ideas carry about 95% of the freight, it wasn't at all hard for me to pick up about 95% of what I needed from all the disciplines and to include use of this knowledge as a standard part of my mental routines. Once you have the ideas, of course, you must continuously practice their use. Like a concert pianist, if you don't practice you can't perform well. So I went through life constantly practicing a multi-disciplinary approach.

Well, this habit has done a lot for me. It's made life more fun. It's made me more constructive. It's made me more helpful to others. It's made me richer than can be explained by any genetic gifts. My mental routine, properly practiced, really helps. Now, there are dangers in it, because it works so well. If you use it you will frequently find when you're with some expert from another discipline—maybe even an expert who is your employer with a vast ability to harm you—that you know more than he does about fitting his specialty to the problem at hand. You'll sometimes see the correct answer when he's missed it. That is a very dangerous position to be in. You can cause enormous offense by being right in a way that causes somebody else to lose face in his own discipline or hierarchy. I never found the perfect way to avoid harm from this serious problem.

Even though I was a good poker player when I was young, I wasn't good enough at pretending when I thought I knew more than my supervisors did. And I didn't try as hard at pretending as would have been prudent. So I gave a lot of offense. Now, I'm generally tolerated as a harmless eccentric who will soon be gone. But, coming up, I had a difficult period to go through. My advice to you is to be better than I was at keeping insights hidden. One of my colleagues, who graduated as number one in his class in law school and clerked at the U.S. Supreme Court, tended as a young lawyer to show that he knew a lot. One day the senior partner he was working under called him in and said, "Listen, Chuck, I want to explain something to you. Your duty is to behave in such a way that the client thinks he's the smartest person in the room. If you have any energy or insight available after that, use it to make your senior partner look like the second smartest person in the room. And only after you've satisfied those two obligations, do you want your light to shine at all." Well, that was a good system for rising in many a large law firm. But it wasn't what I did. I usually moved with the drift of my nature, and if some other people didn't like it, well, I didn't need to be adored by everybody.

Let me further develop the idea that a multi-disciplinary attitude is required if maturity is to be effective. Here I'm following a key idea of the greatest lawyer of antiquity, Marcus Tullius Cicero. Cicero is famous for saying that a man who doesn't know what happened before he's born goes through life like a child. That is a very correct idea. Cicero is right to ridicule somebody so foolish as not to know history. But if you generalize Cicero, as I think one should, there are a lot of other things that one should know in addition to history. And those other things are the big ideas in all the disciplines. And it doesn't help you much just to know something well enough so that on one occasion you can prattle your way to an A in an exam. You have to learn many things in such a way that they're in a mental latticework in your head and you automatically use them the rest of your life. If many of you try that, I solemnly promise that one day most will correctly come to think, "Somehow I've become one of the most effective people in my whole age cohort." And, in contrast, if no effort is made toward such multidisciplinarity, many of the brightest of you who choose this course will live in the middle ranks, or in the shallows.

Another idea that I discovered was encapsulated by that story recounted earlier about the rustic who "wanted to know where he was going to die, so he wouldn't go there." The rustic who had that ridiculous sounding idea had a profound truth in his possession. The way complex adaptive systems work, and the way mental constructs work, problems frequently become easier to solve through "inversion." If you turn problems around into reverse, you often think better. For instance, if you want to help India, the question you should consider asking is not: "How can I help India?" Instead, you should ask: "How can I hurt India?" You find what will do the worst damage, and then try to avoid it. Perhaps the two approaches seem logically the same thing. But those who have mastered algebra know that inversion will often and easily solve problems that otherwise resist solution. And in life, just as in algebra, inversion will help you solve problems that you can't otherwise handle.

Let me use a little inversion now. What will really fail in life? What do we want to avoid? Some answers are easy. For example, sloth and unreliability will fail. If you're unreliable it doesn't matter what your virtues are, you're going to crater immediately. So, faithfully doing what you've engaged to do should be an automatic part of your conduct. Of course you want to avoid sloth and unreliability.

Another thing to avoid is extremely intense ideology because it cabbages up one's mind. You see a lot of it in the worst of the TV preachers. They have different, intense, inconsistent ideas about technical theology, and a lot of them have minds reduced to cabbage. (Audience laughs) And that can happen with political ideology. And if you're young, it's particularly easy to drift into intense and foolish political ideology and never get out. When you announce that you're a loyal member of some cult-like group and you start shouting out the orthodox ideology, what you're doing is pounding it in, pounding it in, pounding it in. You're ruining your mind, sometimes with startling speed. So you want to be very careful with intense ideology. It presents a big danger for the only mind you're ever going to have.

There is a warning example I use whenever I feel threatened by drift toward intense political ideology. Some Scandinavian canoeists succeeded in getting through all the rapids of Scandinavia, and they thought they would continue their success by tackling the big whirlpools in northwest America. The death rate was one hundred percent. A big whirlpool is something you want to avoid. And I think the same is true about intense ideology, particularly when your companions are all true believers.

I have what I call an "iron prescription" that helps me keep sane when I drift toward preferring one intense ideology over another. I feel that I'm not entitled to have an opinion unless I can state the arguments against my position better than the people who are in opposition. I think that I am qualified to speak only when

I've reached that state. This sounds almost as extreme as the "iron prescription" Dean Acheson was fond of attributing to William the Silent of Orange, who roughly said, "It's not necessary to hope in order to persevere." That probably is too tough for most people, although I hope it won't ever become too tough for me. My way of avoiding over-intensity in ideology is easier than Acheson's injunction and worth learning. This business of not drifting into extreme ideology is very, very important in life. If you want to end up wise, heavy ideology is very likely to prevent that outcome.

Another thing that often causes folly and ruin is the "self-serving bias," often subconscious, to which we're all subject. You think that "the true little me" is entitled to do what it wants to do. For instance, why shouldn't the true little me get what it wants by overspending its income? Well, there once was a man who became the most famous composer in the world. But he was utterly miserable most of the time. And one of the reasons was that he always overspent his income. That was Mozart. If Mozart couldn't get by with this kind of asinine conduct, I don't think you should try it. (Audience laughs.)

Generally speaking, envy, resentment, revenge and self-pity are disastrous modes of thought. Self-pity can get pretty close to paranoia. And paranoia is one of the very hardest things to reverse. You do not want to drift into self-pity. I had a friend who carried a thick stack of linen-based cards. And when somebody would make a comment that reflected self-pity, he would slowly and portentously pull out his huge stack of cards, take the top one and hand it to the person. The card said, "Your story has touched my heart. Never have I heard of anyone with as many misfortunes as you." Well, you can say that's waggery, but I suggest it can be mental hygiene. Every time you find you're drifting into self-pity, whatever the cause, even if your child is dying of cancer, self-pity is not going to help. Just give yourself one of my friend's cards. Self-pity is always counterproductive. It's the wrong way to think.

And when you avoid it, you get a great advantage over everybody else, or almost everybody else, because self-pity is a standard response. And you can train yourself out of it.

Of course you also want to get self-serving bias out of your mental routines. Thinking that what's good for you is good for the wider civilization, and rationalizing foolish or evil conduct, based on your subconscious tendency to serve yourself, is a terrible way to think. And you want to drive that out of yourself because you want to be wise not foolish, and good not evil. You also have to allow, in your own cognition and conduct, for the self-serving bias of everybody else, because most people are not going to be very successful at removing such bias, the human condition being what it is. If you don't allow for self-serving bias in the conduct of others, you are, again, a fool.

I watched the brilliant and worthy *Harvard Law Review*-trained general counsel of Salomon Brothers lose his career there. When the able CEO was told that an underling had done something wrong, the general counsel said, "Gee, we don't have any legal duty to report this, but I think it's what we should do. It's our moral duty." The general counsel was technically and morally correct. But his approach didn't persuade. He recommended a very unpleasant thing for the busy CEO to do and the CEO, quite understandably, put the issue off, and put it off, and not with any intent to do wrong. In due course, when powerful regulators resented not having been promptly informed, down went the CEO and the general counsel with him.

The correct persuasive technique in situations like that was given by Ben Franklin. He said, "If you would persuade, appeal to interest, not to reason." The self-serving bias of man is extreme and should have been used in attaining the correct outcome. So the general counsel should have said, "Look, this is likely to erupt into something that will destroy you, take away your money, take away your status, grossly impair your reputation. My recommendation will prevent a likely disaster from which you can't recover." That approach would have worked. You should often appeal to interest, not to reason, even when your motives are lofty.

Another thing to avoid is being subjected to perverse incentives. You don't want to be in a perverse incentive system that's rewarding you if you behave more and more foolishly, or worse and worse. Perverse incentives are so powerful as controllers of human cognition and human behavior that one should avoid their influence. And one of the things you're going to find in at least a few modern law firms is high billable-hour quotas. I could not have lived under billable-hour quotas of 2400 hours a year. That would have caused too many problems for me. I wouldn't have done it. I don't have a solution for the situation some of you will face. You'll have to figure out for yourselves how to handle such significant problems.

Perverse associations are also to be avoided. You particularly want to avoid working directly under somebody you don't admire and don't want to be like. It's dangerous. We're all subject to control to some extent by authority figures, particularly authority figures who are rewarding us. Dealing properly with this danger requires both some talent and will. I coped in my time by identifying people I admired and by maneuvering, mostly without criticizing anybody, so that I was usually working under the right sort of people. A lot of law firms will permit that if you're shrewd enough to work it out with some tact. Generally, your outcome in life will be more satisfactory if you work under people you correctly admire.

Engaging in routines that allow you to maintain objectivity are, of course, very helpful to cognition. We all remember that Darwin paid special attention to disconfirming evidence, particularly when it disconfirmed something he believed and loved. Routines like that are required if a life is to maximize correct thinking. And one also needs checklist routines. They prevent a lot of errors, and not just for pilots. You should not only possess wide-ranging elementary wisdom but also go through mental checklist routines in using it. There is no other procedure that will work as well.

Another idea that I found important is that maximizing non-egality will often work wonders. What do I mean? Well, John Wooden of UCLA presented an instructive example when he was the number one basketball coach in the world. He said to the bottom 5 players, "You don't get to play – you are practice partners." The top seven did almost all the playing. Well, the top seven learned more—remember the importance of the learning machine—because they were doing all the playing. And when he adopted that non-egalitarian system, Wooden won more games than he had won before. I think the game of competitive life often requires maximizing the experience of the people who have the most aptitude and the most determination as learning machines. And if you want the very highest reaches of human achievement, that's where you have to go. You do not want to choose a brain surgeon for your child by drawing straws to select one of fifty applicants, all of whom take turns doing procedures. You don't want your airplanes designed in too egalitarian a fashion. You don't want your Berkshire Hathaways run that way either. You want to provide a lot of playing time for your best players.

I frequently tell the apocryphal story about how Max Planck, after he won the Nobel Prize, went around Germany giving a same standard lecture on the new quantum mechanics. Over time, his chauffeur memorized the lecture and said, "Would you mind, Professor Planck, because it's so boring to stay in our routine, if I gave the lecture in Munich and you just sat in front wearing my chauffeur's hat?" Planck said, "Why not?" And the chauffeur got up and gave this long lecture on quantum mechanics. After which a physics professor stood up and asked a perfectly ghastly question. The speaker said, "Well, I'm surprised that in an advanced city like

Munich I get such an elementary question. I'm going to ask my chauffeur to reply." (Audience laughs.)

Well, the reason I tell that story is not to celebrate the quick wittedness of the protagonist. In this world I think we have two kinds of knowledge: One is Planck knowledge, that of the people who really know. They've paid the dues, they have the aptitude. Then we've got chauffeur knowledge. They have learned to prattle the talk. They may have a big head of hair. They often have fine timbre in their voices. They make a big impression. But in the end what they've got is chauffeur knowledge masquerading as real knowledge. I think I've just described practically every politician in the United States. (Audience claps.) You're going to have the problem in your life of getting as much responsibility as you can into the people with the Planck knowledge and away from the people who have the chauffeur knowledge. And there are huge forces working against you.

My generation has failed you to some extent. More and more, we're delivering to you in California a legislature in which mostly the certified nuts from the left, and the certified nuts from the right, are the ones allowed to serve. And none of them are removable. That's what my generation has done for you. But, you wouldn't like it to be too easy, would you?

Another thing that I have found is that intense interest in any subject is indispensable if you're really going to excel in it. I could force myself to be fairly good in a lot of things, but I couldn't excel in anything in which I didn't have an intense interest. So to some extent you're going to have to do as I did. If at all feasible, you want to maneuver yourself into doing something in which you have an intense interest.

Another thing you have to do is have a lot of assiduity. I like that word because to me it means: "Sit down on your ass until you do it." I've had marvelous partners, full of assiduity, all my life. I think I got them partly because I tried to deserve them and partly because I was shrewd enough to select them, and partly there was some luck. Two partners that I chose for one phase in my life made the following simple agreement when they created a little design / build construction team in the middle of the great depression: "Two-man partnership," they said, "and divide everything equally. And, whenever we're behind in our commitments to other people, we will both work fourteen hours a day, seven days a week, until we're caught up." Well, needless to say, that firm didn't fail. And my partners were widely admired. Simple, old-fashioned ideas like theirs are almost sure to provide a good outcome.

Another thing to cope with is that life is very likely to provide terrible blows, unfair blows. Some people recover, and others don't. And there I think the attitude of Epictetus helps guide one to the right reaction. He thought that every mischance in life, however bad, created an opportunity to behave well. He believed every mischance provided an opportunity to learn something useful. And one's duty was not to become immersed in self-pity, but to utilize each terrible blow in a constructive fashion. His ideas were very sound, influencing the best of the Roman emperors, Marcus Aurelius, and many others over many centuries. And you may remember the epitaph that Epictetus made for himself: "Here lies Epictetus, a slave, maimed in body, the ultimate in poverty, and favored by the Gods." Well, that's the way Epictetus is now remembered: "Favored by the Gods." He was favored because he became wise, became manly, and instructed others, both in his own time and over following centuries.

I've another idea to emphasize in a brief account. My grandfather Munger was the only federal judge in his city for nearly forty years. And I admired him. I'm his namesake. And I'm Confucian enough that even now as I speak I'm thinking, "Well, Judge Munger would be pleased to have me here." All these years after my grandfather is dead, I conceive myself as duty bound to carry the torch for my grandfather's values. One such value was prudence as the servant of duty. Grandfather Munger was a federal judge at a time when there were no pensions for widows of federal judges. So if he didn't save from his income, my grandmother would become a destitute widow. And, besides, net worth would enable him to serve others better. Being the kind of man he was, he underspent his income all his life and left his widow in comfortable circumstances.

But that was not all that his prudence enabled. Along the way, in the '30's, my uncle's tiny bank failed and couldn't reopen without help. My grandfather saved the bank by exchanging over a third of his good assets for horrible bank assets. I've always remembered the event. It reminds me of Houseman's little poem that went something like this:

> *"The thoughts of others*
> *Were light and fleeting,*
> *Of lovers' meeting*
> *Or luck or fame.*
> *Mine were of trouble,*
> *And mine were steady,*
> *And I was ready*
> *When trouble came."*

You may well say, "Who wants to go through life anticipating trouble? Well, I did, trained as I was. I've gone through a long life anticipating trouble. And here I am now, well along in my 84th year. Like Epictetus I've had a favored life. It didn't make me unhappy to anticipate trouble all the time and be ready to perform adequately if trouble came. It didn't hurt me at all. In fact it helped me. So, I quitclaim to you Houseman and Judge Munger.

The last idea that I want to give to you, as you go out into a profession that frequently puts a lot of procedure and some mumbo jumbo into what it does, is that complex bureaucratic procedure does not represent the highest form civilization can reach. One higher form is a seamless, non-bureaucratic web of deserved trust. Not much fancy procedure, just totally reliable people correctly trusting one another. That's the way an operating room works at the Mayo Clinic. If lawyers would there introduce a lot of lawyer-like process, more patients would die. So never forget, when you're a lawyer, that while you may have to sell procedure, you don't always have to buy. In your own life what you want to maximize is a seamless web of deserved trust. And if your proposed marriage contract has 47 pages, my suggestion is that you not enter. (Audience laughs.)

Well, that's enough for one graduation. I hope these ruminations of an old man are useful to you. In the end, I'm speaking toward the only outcome feasible for old Valiant-for-Truth in "Pilgrim's Progress:" "My sword I leave to him who can wield it." (Audience applauds.)

3

THE PSYCHOLOGY OF HUMAN MISJUDGMENT

When I read transcripts of my psychology talks given about fifteen years ago, I realized that I could now create a more logical but much longer "talk," including most of what I had earlier said.

But I immediately saw four big disadvantages.

First, the longer "talk," because it was written out with more logical completeness, would be more boring and confusing to many people than any earlier talk. This would happen because I would use idiosyncratic definitions of psychological tendencies in a manner reminiscent of both psychology textbooks and Euclid. And who reads textbooks for fun or revisits Euclid?

Second, because my formal psychological knowledge came only from skimming three psychology textbooks about fifteen years ago, I know virtually nothing about any academic psychology later developed. Yet, in a longer talk containing guesses, I would be criticizing much academic psychology. This sort of intrusion into a professional territory by an amateur would be sure to be resented by professors who would rejoice in finding my errors and might be prompted to respond to my published criticism by providing theirs. Why should I care about new criticism? Well, who likes new hostility from articulate critics with an information advantage?

Third, a longer version of my ideas would surely draw some disapproval from people formerly disposed to like me. Not only would there be stylistic and substantive objections, but also there would be perceptions of arrogance in an old man who displayed much disregard for conventional wisdom while "popping-off" on a subject in which he had never taken a course. My old Harvard Law classmate, Ed Rothschild, always called such a popping-off "the shoe button complex," named for the condition of a family friend who spoke in oracular style on all subjects after becoming dominant in the shoe button business.

Fourth, I might make a fool of myself.

Despite these four very considerable objections, I decided to publish the much-expanded version. Thus, after many decades in which I have succeeded mostly by restricting action to jobs and methods in which I was unlikely to fail, I have now chosen a course of action in which (1) I have no significant personal benefit to gain, (2) I will surely give some pain to family members and friends, and (3) I may make myself ridiculous. Why am I doing this?

One reason may be that my nature makes me incline toward diagnosing and talking about errors in conventional wisdom. And despite years of being smoothed out by the hard knocks that were inevitable for one with my attitude, I don't believe life ever knocked all the boy's brashness out of the man.

A second reason for my decision is my approval of the attitude of Diogenes when he asked: "Of what use is a philosopher who never offends anybody?"

My third and final reason is the strongest. I have fallen in love with my way of laying out psychology because it has been so useful for me. And so, before I die, I want to imitate to some extent the bequest practices of three characters: the protagonist in John Bunyan's "Pilgrim's Progress," Benjamin Franklin, and my first employer, Ernest Buffett. Bunyan's character, the knight wonderfully named "Old Valiant for Truth," makes the only practical bequest available to him when he says at the end of his life: "My sword I leave to him who can wear it." And like this man, I don't mind if I have misappraised my sword, provided

I have tried to see it correctly, or that many will not wish to try it, or that some who try to wield it may find it serves them not. Ben Franklin, to my great benefit, left behind his autobiography, his *Almanacks*, and much else. And Ernest Buffett did the best he could in the same mode when he left behind "How to Run a Grocery Store and a Few Things I Have Learned about Fishing." Whether or not this last contribution to the genre was the best, I will not say. But I will report that I have now known four generations of Ernest Buffett's descendants and that the results have encouraged my imitation of the founder.

I have long been very interested in standard thinking errors.

However, I was educated in an era wherein the contributions of non-patient-treating psychology to an understanding of misjudgment met little approval from members of the mainstream elite. Instead, interest in psychology was pretty well confined to a group of professors who talked and published mostly for themselves, with much natural detriment from isolation and groupthink.

And so, right after my time at Caltech and Harvard Law School, I possessed a vast ignorance of psychology. Those institutions failed to require knowledge of the subject. And, of course, they couldn't integrate psychology with their other subject matter when they didn't know psychology. Also, like the Nietzsche character who was proud of his lame leg, the institutions were proud of their willful avoidance of "fuzzy" psychology and "fuzzy" psychology professors.

I shared this ignorant mindset for a considerable time. And so did a lot of other people. What are we to think, for instance, of the Caltech course catalogue that for years listed just one psychology professor, self-described as a "Professor of Psychoanalytical Studies," who taught both "Abnormal Psychology" and "Psychoanalysis in Literature"?

Soon after leaving Harvard, I began a long struggle to get rid of the most dysfunctional part of my psychological ignorance. Today, I will describe my long struggle for elementary wisdom and a brief summary of my ending notions. After that, I will give examples, many quite vivid and interesting to me, of both psychology at work and antidotes to psychology-based dysfunction. Then, I will end by asking and answering some general questions raised by what I have said. This will be a long talk.

When I started law practice, I had respect for the power of genetic evolution and appreciation of man's many evolution-based resemblances to less cognitively-gifted animals and insects. I was aware that man was a "social animal," greatly and automatically influenced by behavior he observed in men around him. I also knew that man lived, like barnyard animals and monkeys, in limited-size dominance hierarchies, wherein he tended to respect authority and to like and cooperate with his own hierarchy members while displaying considerable distrust and dislike for competing men not in his own hierarchy.

But this generalized, evolution-based theory structure was inadequate to enable me to cope properly with the cognition I encountered. I was soon surrounded by much extreme irrationality, displayed in patterns and subpatterns. So surrounded, I could see that I was not going to cope as well as I wished with life unless I could acquire a better theory-structure on which to hang my observations and experiences. By then, my craving for more theory had a long history. Partly, I had always loved theory as an aid in puzzle solving and as a means of satisfying my monkey-like curiosity. And, partly, I had found that theory-structure was a superpower in helping one get what one wanted, as I had early discovered in school wherein I had excelled without labor, guided by theory, while many others, without mastery of theory, failed despite monstrous effort. Better theory, I thought, had always worked for me and, if now available, could make me acquire capital and independence faster and better assist everything I loved. And so I slowly developed my own system of psychology, more or less in the self-help style of Ben Franklin and with the determination displayed in the refrain of the nursery story: "'Then I'll do it myself,' said the little red hen."

I was greatly helped in my quest by two turns of mind. First, I had long looked for insight by inversion in the intense manner counseled by the great algebraist, Jacobi: "Invert, always invert." I sought good judgment mostly by collecting instances of bad judgment, then pondering ways to avoid such outcomes. Second, I became so avid a collector of instances of bad judgment that I paid no attention to boundaries between professional territories. After all, why should I search for some tiny, unimportant, hard-to-find new stupidity in my own field when some large, important, easy-to-find stupidity was just over the fence in the other fellow's professional territory? Besides, I could already see that real-world problems didn't neatly lie within territorial boundaries. They jumped right across. And I was dubious of any approach that, when two things were inextricably intertwined and interconnected, would try and think about one thing but not the other. I was afraid, if I tried any such restricted approach, that I would end up, in the immortal words of John L. Lewis, "with no brain at all, just a neck that had haired over."

Pure curiosity, somewhat later, made me wonder how and why destructive cults were often able, over a single long weekend, to turn many tolerably normal people into brainwashed zombies and thereafter keep them in that state indefinitely. I resolved that I would eventually find a good answer to this cult question if I could do so by general reading and much musing.

I also got curious about social insects. It fascinated me that both the fertile female honeybee and the fertile female harvester ant could multiply their quite different normal life expectancies by exactly twenty by engaging in one gangbang in the sky. The

extreme success of the ants also fascinated me—how a few
behavioral algorithms caused such extreme evolutionary success
grounded in extremes of cooperation within the breeding colony
and, almost always, extremes of lethal hostility toward ants outside
the breeding colony, even ants of the same species.

Motivated as I was, by midlife I should probably have turned
to psychology textbooks, but I didn't, displaying my share of the
outcome predicted by the German folk saying: "We are too soon
old and too late smart." However, as I later found out, I may have
been lucky to avoid for so long the academic psychology that
was then laid out in most textbooks. These would not then have
guided me well with respect to cults and were often written as
if the authors were collecting psychology experiments as a boy
collects butterflies—with a passion for more butterflies and more
contact with fellow collectors and little craving for synthesis in
what is already possessed. When I finally got to the psychology
texts, I was reminded of the observation of Jacob Viner, the
great economist, that many an academic is like the truffle hound,
an animal so trained and bred for one narrow purpose that it
is no good at anything else. I was also appalled by hundreds
of pages of extremely nonscientific musing about comparative
weights of nature and nurture in human outcomes. And I found
that introductory psychology texts, by and large, didn't deal
appropriately with a fundamental issue: Psychological tendencies
tend to be both numerous and inseparably intertwined, now and
forever, as they interplay in life. Yet the complex parsing out
of effects from intertwined tendencies was usually avoided by
the writers of the elementary texts. Possibly the authors did not
wish, through complexity, to repel entry of new devotees to their
discipline. And, possibly, the cause of their inadequacy was the one
given by Samuel Johnson in response to a woman who inquired
as to what accounted for his dictionary's misdefinition of the word
"pastern." "Pure ignorance," Johnson replied. And, finally, the
text writers showed little interest in describing standard antidotes

to standard psychology-driven folly, and they thus avoided most discussion of exactly what most interested me.

But academic psychology has some very important merits alongside its defects. I learned this eventually, in the course of general reading, from a book, *Influence*, aimed at a popular audience, by a distinguished psychology professor, Robert Cialdini, at Arizona State, a very big university. Cialdini had made himself into a super-tenured "Regents' Professor" at a very young age by devising, describing, and explaining a vast group of clever experiments in which man manipulated man to his detriment, with all of this made possible by man's intrinsic thinking flaws.

I immediately sent copies of Cialdini's book to all my children. I also gave Cialdini a share of Berkshire stock [Class A] to thank him for what he had done for me and the public. Incidentally, the sale by Cialdini of hundreds of thousands of copies of a book about social psychology was a huge feat, considering that Cialdini didn't claim that he was going to improve your sex life or make you any money.

Part of Cialdini's large book-buying audience came because, like me, it wanted to learn how to become less often tricked by salesmen and circumstances. However, as an outcome not sought by Cialdini, who is a profoundly ethical man, a huge number of his books were bought by salesmen who wanted to learn how to become more effective in misleading customers. Please remember this perverse outcome when my discussion comes to incentive-caused bias as a consequence of the superpower of incentives.

With the push given by Cialdini's book, I soon skimmed through three much used textbooks covering introductory psychology. I also pondered considerably while craving synthesis and taking into account all my previous training and experience. The result was Munger's partial summary of the non-patient-treating, non-nature vs. nurture-weighing parts of nondevelopmental psychology. This material was stolen from its various discoverers (most of whose names I did not even try to learn), often with new descriptions and titles selected to fit Munger's notion of what makes recall easy for Munger, then revised to make Munger's use easy as he seeks to avoid errors.

I will start my summary with a general observation that helps explain what follows. This observation is grounded in what we know about social insects. The limitations inherent in evolution's development of the nervous-system cells that control behavior are beautifully demonstrated by these insects, which often have a mere 100,000 or so cells in their entire nervous systems, compared to man's multiple billions of cells in his brain alone.

Each ant, like each human, is composed of a living physical structure plus behavioral algorithms in its nerve cells. In the ant's case, the behavioral algorithms are few in number and almost entirely genetic in origin. The ant learns a little behavior from experiences, but mostly it merely responds to ten or so stimuli with a few simple responses programmed into its nervous system by its genes.

Naturally, the simple ant behavior system has extreme limitations because of its limited nerve-system repertoire. For instance, one type of ant, when it smells a pheromone given off by a dead ant's body in the hive, immediately responds by cooperating with other ants in carrying the dead body out of the hive. And Harvard's great E.O. Wilson performed one of the best psychology experiments ever done when he painted dead-ant pheromone on a live ant. Quite naturally, the other ants dragged this useful live ant out of the hive even though it kicked and otherwise protested throughout the entire process. Such is the brain of the ant. It has a simple program of responses that generally work out all right, but which are imprudently used by rote in many cases.

Another type of ant demonstrates that the limited brain of ants can be misled by circumstances as well as by clever manipulation from other creatures. The brain of this ant contains a simple behavioral program that directs the ant, when walking, to follow the ant ahead. And when these ants stumble into walking in a big circle, they sometimes walk round and round until they perish.

It seems obvious, to me at least, that the human brain must often operate counterproductively just like the ant's, from unavoidable oversimplicity in its mental process, albeit usually in trying to solve problems more difficult than those faced by ants that don't have to design airplanes.

The perception system of man clearly demonstrates just such an unfortunate outcome. Man is easily fooled, either by the cleverly thought out manipulation of man, by circumstances occurring by accident, or by very effective manipulation practices that man has stumbled into during "practice evolution" and kept in place because they work so well. One such outcome is caused by a quantum effect in human perception. If stimulus is kept below a certain level, it does not get through. And, for this reason, a magician was able to make the Statue of Liberty disappear after a certain amount of magician lingo expressed in the dark. The audience was not aware that it was sitting on a platform that was rotating so slowly, below man's sensory threshold, that no one could feel the acceleration implicit in the considerable rotation. When a surrounding curtain was then opened in the place on the platform where the Statue had earlier appeared, it seemed to have disappeared.

And even when perception does get through to man's brain, it is often misweighted, because what is registered in perception is in shockingness of apparent contrast, not the standard scientific units that make possible science and good engineering.

A magician demonstrates this sort of contrast-based error in your nervous system when he removes your wristwatch without your feeling it. As he does this, he applies pressure of touch on your wrist that you would sense if it was the only pressure of touch you were experiencing. But he has concurrently applied other intense pressure of touch on your body, but not on your wrist, "swamping" the wrist pressure by creating a high-contrast touch pressure elsewhere. This high contrast takes the wrist pressure below perception.

Some psychology professors like to demonstrate the inadequacy of contrast-based perception by having students put one hand in a bucket of hot water and one hand in a bucket of cold water. They are then suddenly asked to remove both hands and place them in a single bucket of room-temperature water. Now, with both hands in the same water, one hand feels as if it has just been put in cold water and the other hand feels as if it has just been placed in hot water. When one thus sees perception so easily fooled by mere contrast, where a simple temperature gauge would make no error, and realizes that cognition mimics perception in being misled by mere contrast, he is well on the way toward understanding, not only how magicians fool one, but also how life will fool one. This can occur, through deliberate human manipulation or otherwise, if one doesn't take certain precautions against often-wrong effects from generally useful tendencies in his perception and cognition.

Man's—often wrong but generally useful—psychological tendencies are quite numerous and quite different. The natural consequence of this profusion of tendencies is the grand general principle of social psychology: cognition is ordinarily situation-dependent so that different situations often cause different conclusions, even when the same person is thinking in the same general subject area.

With this introductory instruction from ants, magicians, and the grand general principle of social psychology, I will next simply number and list psychology-based tendencies that, while generally useful, often mislead. Discussion of errors from each tendency will come later, together with description of some antidotes to errors, followed by some general discussion. Here are the tendencies:

One: Reward and Punishment Superresponse Tendency

Two: Liking/Loving Tendency

Three: Disliking/Hating Tendency

Four: Doubt-Avoidance Tendency

Five: Inconsistency-Avoidance Tendency

Six: Curiosity Tendency

Seven: Kantian Fairness Tendency

Eight: Envy/Jealousy Tendency

Nine: Reciprocation Tendency

Ten: Influence-from-Mere-Association Tendency

Eleven: Simple, Pain-Avoiding Psychological Denial

Twelve: Excessive Self-Regard Tendency

Thirteen: Overoptimism Tendency

Fourteen: Deprival-Superreaction Tendency

Fifteen: Social-Proof Tendency

Sixteen: Contrast-Misreaction Tendency

Seventeen: Stress-Influence Tendency

Eighteen: Availability-Misweighing Tendency

Nineteen: Use-It-or-Lose-It Tendency

Twenty: Drug-Misinfluence Tendency

Twenty-One: Senescence-Misinfluence Tendency

Twenty-Two: Authority-Misinfluence Tendency

Twenty-Three: Twaddle Tendency

Twenty-Four: Reason-Respecting Tendency

Twenty-Five: Lollapalooza Tendency—The Tendency to Get Extreme Consequences from Confluences of Psychological Tendencies Acting in Favor of a Particular Outcome

ONE:
Reward and Punishment
Superresponse Tendency

I place this tendency first in my discussion because almost everyone thinks he fully recognizes how important incentives and disincentives are in changing cognition and behavior. But this is not often so. For instance, I think I've been in the top five percent of my age cohort almost all my adult life in understanding the power of incentives, and yet I've always underestimated that power. Never a year passes but I get some surprise that pushes a little further my appreciation of incentive superpower.

One of my favorite cases about the power of incentives is the Federal Express case. The integrity of the Federal Express system requires that all packages be shifted rapidly among airplanes in one central airport each night. And the system has no integrity for the customers if the night work shift can't accomplish its assignment fast. And Federal Express had one hell of a time getting the night shift to do the right thing. They tried moral suasion. They tried everything in the world without luck. And, finally, somebody got the happy thought that it was foolish to pay the night shift by the hour when what the employer wanted was not maximized billable hours of employee service but fault-free, rapid performance of a particular task. Maybe, this person thought, if they paid the employees per shift and let all night shift employees go home when all the planes were loaded, the system would work better. And, lo and behold, that solution worked.

Early in the history of Xerox, Joe Wilson, who was then in the government, had a similar experience. He had to go back to Xerox because he couldn't understand why its new machine was selling so poorly in relation to its older and inferior machine. When he got back to Xerox, he found out that the commission arrangement with the salesmen gave a large and perverse incentive to push the inferior machine on customers, who deserved a better result.

And then there is the case of Mark Twain's cat that, after a bad experience with a hot stove, never again sat on a hot stove, or a cold stove either.

We should also heed the general lesson implicit in the injunction of Ben Franklin in *Poor Richard's Almanack*: "If you would persuade, appeal to interest and not to reason." This maxim is a wise guide to a great and simple precaution in life: Never, ever, think about something else when you should be thinking about the power of incentives. I once saw a very smart house counsel for a major investment bank lose his job, with no moral fault, because he ignored the lesson in this maxim of Franklin. This counsel failed to persuade his client because he told him his moral duty, as correctly conceived by the counsel, without also telling the client in vivid terms that he was very likely to be clobbered to smithereens if he didn't behave as his counsel recommended. As a result, both client and counsel lost their careers.

We should also remember how a foolish and willful ignorance of the superpower of rewards caused Soviet communists to get their final result as described by one employee: "They pretend to pay us and we pretend to work." Perhaps the most important rule in management is "Get the incentives right."

But there is some limit to a desirable emphasis on incentive superpower. One case of excess emphasis happened at Harvard, where B. F. Skinner, a psychology professor, finally made himself ridiculous. At one time, Skinner may have been the best-known psychology professor in the world. He partly deserved his peak reputation because his early experiments using rats and pigeons were ingenious, and his results were both counterintuitive and important. With incentives, he could cause more behavior change, culminating in conditioned reflexes in his rats and pigeons, than he could in any other way. He made obvious the extreme stupidity, in dealing with children or employees, of rewarding behavior one didn't want more of. Using food rewards, he even caused strong superstitions, predesigned by himself, in his pigeons. He demonstrated again and again a great recurring, generalized behavioral algorithm in nature: "Repeat behavior that works." He also demonstrated that prompt rewards worked much better than delayed rewards in changing and maintaining behavior. And, once his rats and pigeons had conditioned reflexes, caused by food rewards, he found what withdrawal pattern of rewards kept the reflexive behavior longest in place: random distribution. With this result, Skinner thought he had pretty well explained man's misgambling compulsion whereunder he often foolishly proceeds to ruin. But, as we shall later see when we discuss other psychological tendencies that contribute to misgambling compulsion, he was only partly right. Later, Skinner lost most of his personal reputation (a) by overclaiming for incentive superpower to the point of thinking he could create a human utopia with it and (b) by displaying hardly any recognition of the power of the rest of psychology. He thus behaved like one of Jacob Viner's truffle hounds as he tried to explain everything with incentive effects. Nonetheless, Skinner was right in his main idea: Incentives are superpowers. The outcome of his basic experiments will always remain in high repute in the annals of experimental science. And his method of monomaniacal reliance on rewards, for many decades after his death, did more good than anything else in improving autistic children.

When I was at Harvard Law School, the professors sometimes talked about an overfocused, Skinner-like professor at Yale Law School. They used to say: "Poor old Eddie Blanchard, he thinks declaratory judgments will cure cancer." Well, that's the way Skinner got with his very extreme emphasis on incentive superpower. I always call the "Johnny-one-note" turn of mind that eventually so diminished Skinner's reputation the man-with-a-hammer tendency, after the folk saying: "To a man with only a hammer every problem looks pretty much like a nail." Man-with-a-hammer tendency does not exempt smart people like Blanchard and Skinner. And it won't exempt you if you don't watch out. I will return to man-with-a-hammer tendency at various times in this talk because, fortunately, there are effective antidotes that reduce the ravages of what pretty much ruined the personal reputation of the brilliant Skinner.

One of the most important consequences of incentive superpower is what I call "incentive-caused bias." A man has an acculturated nature making him a pretty decent fellow, and yet, driven both consciously and subconsciously by incentives, he drifts into immoral behavior in order to get what he wants, a result he facilitates by rationalizing his bad behavior, like the salesmen at Xerox who harmed customers in order to maximize their sales commissions.

Here, my early education involved a surgeon who over the years sent bushel baskets full of normal gall bladders down to the pathology lab in the leading hospital in Lincoln, Nebraska, my grandfather's town. And, with that permissive quality control for which community hospitals are famous, many years after this surgeon should've been removed from the medical staff, he was. One of the doctors who participated in the removal was a family friend, and I asked him: "Did this surgeon think, 'Here's a way for me to exercise my talents'—this guy was very skilled technically—'and make a high living by doing a few maimings and murders every year in the course of routine fraud?'" And my friend answered: "Hell no, Charlie. He thought that the gall bladder was the source of all medical evil, and, if you really loved your patients, you couldn't get that organ out rapidly enough."

Now that's an extreme case, but in lesser strength, the cognitive drift of that surgeon is present in every profession and in every human being. And it causes perfectly terrible behavior. Consider the presentations of brokers selling commercial real estate and businesses. I've never seen one that I thought was even within hailing distance of objective truth. In my long life, I have never seen a management consultant's report that didn't end with the same advice: "This problem needs more management consulting services." Widespread incentive-caused bias requires that one should often distrust, or take with a grain of salt, the advice of one's professional advisor, even if he is an engineer. The general antidotes here are: (1) especially fear professional advice when it is especially good for the advisor; (2) learn and use the basic elements of your advisor's trade as you deal with your advisor; and (3) double check, disbelieve, or replace much of what you're told, to the degree that seems appropriate after objective thought.

The power of incentives to cause rationalized, terrible behavior is also demonstrated by Defense Department procurement history. After the Defense Department had much truly awful experience with misbehaving contractors motivated under contracts paying on a cost-plus-a-percentage-of-cost basis, the reaction of our republic was to make it a crime for a contracting officer in the Defense Department to sign such a contract, and not only a crime, but a felony.

And, by the way, although the government was right to create this new felony, much of the way the rest of the world is run, including the operation of many law firms and a lot of other firms, is still under what is, in essence, a cost-plus-a-percentage-of-cost reward system. And human nature, bedeviled by incentive-caused bias, causes a lot of ghastly abuse under these standard incentive patterns of the world. And many of the people who are behaving terribly you would be glad to have married into your family, compared to what you're otherwise likely to get.

Now there are huge implications from the fact that the human mind is put together this way. One implication is that people who create things like cash registers, which make dishonest behavior hard to accomplish, are some of the effective saints of our civilization because, as Skinner so well knew, bad behavior is intensely habit-forming when it is rewarded. And so the cash register was a great moral instrument when it was created. And, by the way, Patterson, the great evangelist of the cash register, knew that from his own experience. He had a little store, and his employees were stealing him blind, so that he never made any money. Then people sold him a couple of cash registers, and his store went to profit immediately. He promptly closed the store and went into the cash register business, creating what became the mighty National Cash Register Company, one of the glories of its time. "Repeat behavior that works" is a behavioral guide that really succeeded for Patterson, after he applied one added twist. And so did high moral cognition. An eccentric, inveterate do-gooder (except when destroying competitors, all of which he regarded as would-be patent thieves), Patterson, like Carnegie, pretty well gave away all his money to charity before he died, always pointing out that "shrouds have no pockets." So great was the contribution of Patterson's cash register to civilization, and so effectively did he improve the cash register and spread its use, that in the end, he probably deserved the epitaph chosen for the Roman poet Horace: "I did not completely die."

The strong tendency of employees to rationalize bad conduct in order to get rewards requires many antidotes in addition to the good cash control promoted by Patterson. Perhaps the most important of these antidotes is use of sound accounting theory and practice. This was seldom better demonstrated than at Westinghouse, which had a subsidiary that made loans having no connection to the rest of Westinghouse's businesses. The officers of Westinghouse, perhaps influenced by envy of General Electric, wanted to expand profits from loans to outsiders. Under Westinghouse's accounting practice, provisions for future credit losses on these loans depended largely on the past credit experience of its lending subsidiary, which mainly made loans unlikely to cause massive losses.

Now there are two special classes of loans that naturally cause much trouble for lenders. The first is ninety-five percent-of-value construction loans to any kind of real estate developer, and the second is any kind of construction loan on a hotel. So, naturally, if one was willing to loan approximately ninety-five percent of the real cost to a developer constructing a hotel, the loan would bear a much-higher-than-normal interest rate because the credit-loss danger would be much higher than normal. So, sound accounting for Westinghouse in making a big, new mass of ninety-five percent-of-value construction loans to hotel developers would have been to report almost no profit, or even a loss, on each loan until, years later, the loan became clearly worth par. But Westinghouse instead plunged into big-time construction lending on hotels, using accounting that made its lending officers look good because it showed extremely high starting income from loans that were very inferior to the loans from which the company had suffered small credit losses in the past. This terrible accounting was allowed by both international and outside accountants for Westinghouse as they displayed the conduct predicted by the refrain: "Whose bread I eat, his song I sing."

The result was billions of dollars of losses. Who was at fault? The guy from the refrigerator division, or some similar division, who as lending officer was suddenly in charge of loans to hotel developers? Or the accountants and other senior people who tolerated a nearly insane incentive structure, almost sure to trigger incentive-caused bias in a lending officer? My answer puts most blame on the accountants and other senior people who created the accounting system. These people became the equivalent of an armored car cash-carrying service that suddenly decided to dispense with vehicles and have unarmed midgets hand-carry its customers' cash through slums in open bushel baskets.

I wish I could tell you that this sort of thing no longer happens, but this is not so. After Westinghouse blew up, General Electric's

Kidder Peabody subsidiary put a silly computer program in place that allowed a bond trader to show immense fictional profits. And after that, much accounting became even worse, perhaps reaching its nadir at Enron.

And so incentive-caused bias is a huge, important thing, with highly important antidotes, like the cash register and a sound accounting system. But when I came years ago to the psychology texts, I found that, while they were about one thousand pages long, there was little therein that dealt with incentive-caused bias and no mention of Patterson or sound accounting systems. Somehow incentive-caused bias and its antidotes pretty well escaped the standard survey courses in psychology, even though incentive-caused bias had long been displayed prominently in much of the world's great literature, and antidotes to it had long existed in standard business routines. In the end, I concluded that when something was obvious in life but not easily demonstrable in certain kinds of easy-to-do, repeatable academic experiments, the truffle hounds of psychology very often missed it.

In some cases, other disciplines showed more interest in psychological tendencies than did psychology, at least as explicated in psychology textbooks. For instance, economists, speaking from the employer's point of view, have long had a name for the natural results of incentive-caused bias: "agency cost." As the name implies, the economists have typically known that, just as grain is always lost to rats, employers always lose to employees who improperly think of themselves first. Employer-installed antidotes include tough internal audit systems and severe public punishment for identified miscreants, as well as misbehavior-preventing routines and such machines as cash registers. From the employee's point of view, incentive-caused bias quite naturally causes opposing abuse from the employer: the sweatshop, the unsafe work place, etc. And these bad results for employees have antidotes not only in pressure from unions but also in government action, such as wage and hour laws, work-place-safety rules, measures fostering unionization, and workers' compensation systems. Given the opposing psychology-induced strains that naturally occur in employment because of incentive-caused bias on both sides of the relationship, it is no wonder the Chinese are so much into Yin and Yang.

The inevitable ubiquity of incentive-caused bias has vast, generalized consequences. For instance, a sales force living only on commissions will be much harder to keep moral than one under less pressure from the compensation arrangement. On the other hand, a purely commissioned sales force may well be more efficient per dollar spent. Therefore, difficult decisions involving trade-offs are common in creating compensation arrangements in the sales function.

The extreme success of free-market capitalism as an economic system owes much to its prevention of many of bad effects from incentive-caused bias. Most capitalist owners in a vast web of free-market economic activity are selected for ability by surviving in a brutal competition with other owners and have a strong incentive to prevent all waste in operations within their ownership. After all, they live on the difference between their competitive prices and their overall costs and their businesses will perish if costs exceed sales. Replace such owners by salaried employees of the state and you will normally get a substantial reduction in overall efficiency as each employee who replaces an owner is subject to incentive-caused bias as he determines what service he will give in exchange for his salary and how much he will yield to peer pressure from many fellow employees who do not desire his creation of any strong performance model.

Another generalized consequence of incentive-caused bias is that man tends to "game" all human systems, often displaying great ingenuity in wrongly serving himself at the expense of others. Anti-gaming features, therefore, constitute a huge and necessary part of almost all system design. Also needed in system design is an admonition: Dread, and avoid as much as you can, rewarding people for what can be easily faked. Yet our legislators and judges, usually including many lawyers educated in eminent universities, often ignore this injunction. And society consequently pays a huge price in the deterioration of behavior and efficiency, as well as the incurrence of unfair costs and wealth transfers. If education were improved, with psychological reality becoming better taught and assimilated, better system design might well come out of our legislatures and courts.

Of course, money is now the main reward that drives habits. A monkey can be trained to seek and work for an intrinsically worthless token, as if it were a banana, if the token is routinely exchangeable for a banana. So it is also with humans working for money—only more so, because human money is exchangeable for many desired things in addition to food, and one ordinarily gains status from either holding or spending it. Moreover, a rich person will often, through habit, work or connive energetically for more money long after he has almost no real need for more. Averaged out, money is a mainspring of modern civilization, having little precedent in the behavior of nonhuman animals. Money rewards are also intertwined with other forms of reward. For instance, some people use money to buy status and others use status to get money, while still others sort of do both things at the same time.

Although money is the main driver among rewards, it is not the only reward that works. People also change their behavior and cognition for sex, friendship, companionship, advancement in status, and other nonmonetary items.

"Granny's Rule" provides another example of reward superpower, so extreme in its effects that it must be mentioned here. You can successfully manipulate your own behavior with this rule, even if you are using as rewards items that you already possess! Indeed, consultant Ph. D. psychologists often urge business organizations to improve their reward systems by teaching executives to use "Granny's Rule" to govern their own daily behavior. Granny's Rule, to be specific, is the requirement that children eat their carrots before they get dessert. And the business version requires that executives force themselves daily to first do their unpleasant and necessary tasks before rewarding themselves by proceeding to their pleasant tasks. Given reward superpower, this practice is wise and sound. Moreover, the rule can also be used in the nonbusiness part of life. The emphasis on daily use of this practice is not accidental. The consultants well know, after the teaching of Skinner, that prompt rewards work best.

Punishments, of course, also strongly influence behavior and cognition, although not so flexibly and wonderfully as rewards. For instance, illegal price fixing was fairly common in America when it was customarily punished by modest fines. Then, after a few prominent business executives were removed from their eminent positions and sent to federal prisons, price-fixing behavior was greatly reduced.

Military and naval organizations have very often been extreme in using punishment to change behavior, probably because they needed to cause extreme behavior. Around the time of Caesar, there was a European tribe that, when the assembly horn blew, always killed the last warrior to reach his assigned place, and no one enjoyed fighting this tribe. And George Washington hanged farm-boy deserters forty feet high as an example to others who might contemplate desertion.

TWO:
Liking/Loving Tendency

A newly hatched baby goose is programmed, through the economy of its genetic program, to "love" and follow the first creature that is nice to it, which is almost always its mother. But, if the mother goose is not present right after the hatching, and a man is there instead, the gosling will "love" and follow the man, who becomes a sort of substitute mother.

Somewhat similarly, a newly arrived human is "born to like and love" under the normal and abnormal triggering outcomes for its kind. Perhaps the strongest inborn tendency to love—ready to be triggered—is that of the human mother for its child. On the other hand, the similar "child-loving" behavior of a mouse can be eliminated by the deletion of a single gene, which suggests there is some sort of triggering gene in a mother mouse as well as in a gosling.

Each child, like a gosling, will almost surely come to like and love, not only as driven by its sexual nature, but also in social groups not limited to its genetic or adoptive "family." Current extremes of romantic love almost surely did not occur in man's remote past. Our early human ancestors were surely more like apes triggered into mating in a pretty mundane fashion.

And what will a man naturally come to like and love, apart from his parent, spouse and child? Well, he will like and love being liked and loved. And so many a courtship competition will be won by a person displaying exceptional devotion, and man will generally strive, lifelong, for the affection and approval of many people not related to him.

One very practical consequence of Liking/Loving Tendency is that it acts as a conditioning device that makes the liker or lover tend (1) to ignore faults of, and comply with wishes of, the object of his affection, (2) to favor people, products, and actions merely associated with the object of his affection (as we shall see when we get to "Influence-from-Mere-Association Tendency," and (3) to distort other facts to facilitate love.

The phenomenon of liking and loving causing admiration also works in reverse. Admiration also causes or intensifies liking or love. With this "feedback mode" in place, the consequences are often extreme, sometimes even causing deliberate self-destruction to help what is loved.

Liking or loving, intertwined with admiration in a feedback mode, often has vast practical consequences in areas far removed from sexual attachments. For instance, a man who is so constructed that he loves admirable persons and ideas with a special intensity has a huge advantage in life. This blessing came to both Buffett and myself in large measure, sometimes from the same persons and ideas. One common, beneficial example for us both was Warren's uncle, Fred Buffett, who cheerfully did the endless grocery-store work that Warren and I ended up admiring from a safe distance. Even now, after I have known so many other people, I doubt if it is possible to be a nicer man than Fred Buffett was, and he changed me for the better.

There are large social policy implications in the amazingly good consequences that ordinarily come from people likely to trigger extremes of love and admiration boosting each other in a feedback mode. For instance, it is obviously desirable to attract a lot of lovable, admirable people into the teaching profession.

THREE:
Disliking/Hating Tendency

In a pattern obverse to Liking/Loving Tendency, the newly arrived human is also "born to dislike and hate" as triggered by normal and abnormal triggering forces in its life. It is the same with most apes and monkeys.

As a result, the long history of man contains almost continuous war. For instance, most American Indian tribes warred incessantly, and some tribes would occasionally bring captives home to women so that all could join in the fun of torturing captives to death. Even with the spread of religion, and the advent of advanced civilization, much modern war remains pretty savage. But we also get what we observe in present-day Switzerland and the United States, wherein the clever political arrangements of man "channel" the hatreds and dislikings of individuals and groups into nonlethal patterns including elections.

But the dislikings and hatreds never go away completely. Born into man, these driving tendencies remain strong. Thus, we get maxims like the one from England: "Politics is the art of marshalling hatreds." And we also get the extreme popularity of very negative political advertising in the United States.

At the family level, we often see one sibling hate his other siblings and litigate with them endlessly if he can afford it. Indeed, a wag named Buffett has repeatedly explained to me that "a major difference between rich and poor people is that the rich people can spend their lives suing their relatives." My father's law practice in Omaha was full of such intrafamily hatreds. And when I got to the Harvard Law School and its professors taught me "property law" with no mention of sibling rivalry in the family business, I appraised the School as a pretty unrealistic place that wore "blinders" like the milk-wagon horses of yore. My current guess is that sibling rivalry has not yet made it into property law as taught at Harvard.

Disliking/Hating Tendency also acts as a conditioning device that makes the disliker/hater tend to (1) ignore virtues in the object of dislike, (2) dislike people, products, and actions merely associated with the object of his dislike, and (3) distort other facts to facilitate hatred.

Distortion of that kind is often so extreme that miscognition is shockingly large. When the World Trade Center was destroyed, many Pakistanis immediately concluded that the Hindus did it, while many Muslims concluded that the Jews did it. Such factual distortions often make mediation between opponents locked in hatred either difficult or impossible. Mediations between Israelis and Palestinians are difficult because facts in one side's history overlap very little with facts from the other side's.

FOUR:
Doubt-Avoidance Tendency

The brain of man is programmed with a tendency to quickly remove doubt by reaching some decision.

It is easy to see how evolution would make animals, over the eons, drift toward such quick elimination of doubt. After all, the one thing that is surely counterproductive for a prey animal that is threatened by a predator is to take a long time in deciding what to do. And so man's Doubt-Avoidance Tendency is quite consistent with the history of his ancient, nonhuman ancestors.

So pronounced is the tendency in man to quickly remove doubt by reaching some decision that behavior to counter the tendency is required from judges and jurors. Here, delay before decision making is forced. And one is required to so comport himself, prior to conclusion time, so that he is wearing a "mask" of objectivity. And the "mask" works to help real objectivity along, as we shall see when we next consider man's Inconsistency-Avoidance Tendency.

Of course, once one has recognized that man has a strong Doubt-Avoidance Tendency, it is logical to believe that at least some leaps of religious faith are greatly boosted by this tendency. Even if one is satisfied that his own faith comes from revelation, one still must account for the inconsistent faiths of others. And man's Doubt-Avoidance Tendency is almost surely a big part of the answer.

What triggers Doubt-Avoidance Tendency? Well, an unthreatened man, thinking of nothing in particular, is not being prompted to remove doubt through rushing to some decision. As we shall see later when we get to Social-Proof Tendency and Stress-Influence Tendency, what usually triggers Doubt-Avoidance Tendency is some combination of (1) puzzlement and (2) stress. And both of these factors naturally occur in facing religious issues.

Thus, the natural state of most men is in some form of religion. And this is what we observe.

FIVE:
Inconsistency-Avoidance Tendency

The brain of man conserves programming space by being reluctant to change, which is a form of inconsistency avoidance. We see this in all human habits, constructive and destructive. Few people can list a lot of bad habits that they have eliminated, and some people cannot identify even one of these. Instead, practically everyone has a great many bad habits he has long maintained despite their being known as bad. Given this situation, it is not too much in many cases to appraise early-formed habits as destiny. When Marley's miserable ghost says, "I wear the chains I forged in life," he is talking about chains of habit that were too light to be felt before they became too strong to be broken.

The rare life that is wisely lived has in it many good habits maintained and many bad habits avoided or cured. And the great rule that helps here is again from Franklin's *Poor Richard's Almanack*: "An ounce of prevention is worth a pound of cure." What Franklin is here indicating, in part, is that Inconsistency-Avoidance Tendency makes it much easier to prevent a habit than to change it.

Also tending to be maintained in place by the anti-change tendency of the brain are one's previous conclusions, human loyalties, reputational identity, commitments, accepted role in a civilization, etc. It is not entirely clear why evolution would program into man's brain an anti-change mode alongside his tendency to quickly remove doubt. My guess is the anti-change mode was significantly caused by a combination of the following factors:

(1)   It facilitated faster decisions when speed of decision was an important contribution to the survival of nonhuman ancestors that were prey.

(2)   It facilitated the survival advantage that our ancestors gained by cooperating in groups, which would have been more difficult to do if everyone was always changing responses.

(3)   It was the best form of solution that evolution could get to in the limited number of generations between the start of literacy and today's complex modern life.

It is easy to see that a quickly reached conclusion, triggered by Doubt-Avoidance Tendency, when combined with a tendency to resist any change in that conclusion, will naturally cause a lot of errors in cognition for modern man. And so it observably works out. We all deal much with others whom we correctly diagnose as imprisoned in poor conclusions that are maintained by mental habits they formed early and will carry to their graves.

So great is the bad-decision problem caused by Inconsistency-Avoidance Tendency that our courts have adopted important strategies against it. For instance, before making decisions, judges and juries are required to hear long and skillful presentations of evidence and argument from the side they will not naturally favor, given their ideas in place. And this helps prevent considerable bad thinking from "first conclusion bias." Similarly, other modern decision makers will often force groups to consider skillful counterarguments before making decisions.

And proper education is one long exercise in augmentation of high cognition so that our wisdom becomes strong enough to destroy wrong thinking maintained by resistance to change. As Lord Keynes pointed out about his exalted intellectual group at one of the greatest universities in the world, it was not the intrinsic difficulty of new ideas that prevented their acceptance. Instead, the new ideas were not accepted because they were inconsistent with old ideas in place. What Keynes was reporting is that the human mind works a lot like the human egg. When one sperm gets into a human egg, there's an automatic shut-off device that bars any other sperm from getting in. The human mind tends strongly toward the same sort of result.

And so, people tend to accumulate large mental holdings of fixed conclusions and attitudes that are not often reexamined or changed, even though there is plenty of good evidence that they are wrong. Moreover, this doesn't just happen in social science departments, like the one that once thought Freud should serve as the only choice as a psychology teacher for Caltech. Holding to old errors even happens, although with less frequency and severity, in hard science departments. We have no less an authority for this than Max Planck, Nobel laureate, finder of "Planck's constant." Planck is famous not only for his science but also for saying that even in physics the radically new ideas are seldom really accepted by the old guard. Instead, said Planck, the progress is made by a new generation that comes along, less brain-blocked by its previous conclusions. Indeed, precisely this sort of brain-blocking happened to a degree in Einstein. At his peak, Einstein was a great destroyer of his own ideas, but an older Einstein never accepted the full implications of quantum mechanics.

One of the most successful users of an antidote to first conclusion bias was Charles Darwin. He trained himself, early, to intensively consider any evidence tending to disconfirm any hypothesis of his, more so if he thought his hypothesis was a particularly good one. The opposite of what Darwin did is now called confirmation bias, a term of opprobrium. Darwin's practice came from his acute recognition of man's natural cognitive faults arising from Inconsistency-Avoidance Tendency. He provides a great example of psychological insight correctly used to advance some of the finest mental work ever done.

Inconsistency-Avoidance Tendency has many good effects in civilization. For instance, rather than act inconsistently with public commitments, new or old public identities, etc., most people are more loyal in their roles in life as priests, physicians, citizens, soldiers, spouses, teachers, employees, etc.

One corollary of Inconsistency-Avoidance Tendency is that a person making big sacrifices in the course of assuming a new identity will intensify his devotion to the new identity. After all, it would be quite inconsistent behavior to make a large sacrifice for something that was no good. And thus civilization has invented many tough and solemn initiation ceremonies, often public in nature, that intensify new commitments made.

Tough initiation ceremonies can intensify bad contact as well as good. The loyalty of the new, "made-man" mafia member, or of the military officer making the required "blood oath" of loyalty to Hitler, was boosted through the triggering of Inconsistency-Avoidance Tendency.

Moreover, the tendency will often make man a "patsy" of manipulative "compliance-practitioners," who gain advantage from triggering his subconscious Inconsistency-Avoidance Tendency. Few people demonstrated this process better than Ben Franklin. As he was rising from obscurity in Philadelphia and wanted the approval of some important man, Franklin would often maneuver that man into doing Franklin some unimportant favor, like lending Franklin a book. Thereafter, the man would admire and trust Franklin more because a nonadmired and nontrusted Franklin would be inconsistent with the appraisal implicit in lending Franklin the book.

During the Korean War, this technique of Franklin's was the most important feature of the Chinese brainwashing system that was used on enemy prisoners. Small step by small step, the technique often worked better than torture in altering prisoner cognition in favor of Chinese captors.

The practice of Franklin, whereunder he got approval from someone by maneuvering him into treating Franklin favorably, works viciously well in reverse. When one is maneuvered into deliberately hurting some other person, one will tend to disapprove or even hate that person. This effect, from Inconsistency-

Avoidance Tendency, accounts for the insight implicit in the saying: "A man never forgets where he has buried the hatchet." The effect accounts for much prisoner abuse by guards, increasing their dislike and hatred for prisoners that exists as a consequence of the guards' reciprocation of hostility from prisoners who are treated like animals. Given the psychology-based hostility natural in prisons between guards and prisoners, an intense, continuous effort should be made (1) to prevent prisoner abuse from starting and (2) to stop it instantly when it starts because it will grow by feeding on itself, like a cluster of infectious disease. More psychological acuity on this subject, aided by more insightful teaching, would probably improve the overall effectiveness of the U.S. Army.

So strong is Inconsistency-Avoidance Tendency that it will often prevail after one has merely pretended to have some identity, habit, or conclusion. Thus, for a while, many an actor sort of believes he is Hamlet, Prince of Denmark. And many a hypocrite is improved by his pretensions of virtue. And many a judge and juror, while pretending objectivity, is gaining objectivity. And many a trial lawyer or other advocate comes to believe what he formerly only pretended to believe.

While Inconsistency-Avoidance Tendency, with its "status quo bias," immensely harms sound education, it also causes much benefit. For instance, a near-ultimate inconsistency would be to teach something to others that one did not believe true. And so, in clinical medical education, the learner is forced to "see one, do one, and then teach one," with the teaching pounding the learning into the teacher. Of course, the power of teaching to influence the cognition of the teacher is not always a benefit to society. When such power flows into political and cult evangelism, there are often bad consequences.

For instance, modern education often does much damage when young students are taught dubious political notions and then enthusiastically push these notions on the rest of us. The pushing seldom convinces others. But as students pound into their mental habits what they are pushing out, the students are often permanently damaged. Educational institutions that create a climate where much of this goes on are, I think, irresponsible. It is important not to thus put one's brain in chains before one has come anywhere near his full potentiality as a rational person.

SIX:
Curiosity Tendency

There is a lot of innate curiosity in mammals, but its nonhuman version is highest among apes and monkeys. Man's curiosity, in turn, is much stronger than that of his simian relatives. In advanced human civilization, culture greatly increases the effectiveness of curiosity in advancing knowledge. For instance, Athens (including its colony, Alexandria) developed much math and science out of pure curiosity while the Romans made almost no contribution to either math or science. They instead concentrated their attention on the "practical" engineering of mines, roads, aqueducts, etc. Curiosity, enhanced by the best of modern education (which is by definition a minority part in many places), much helps man to prevent or reduce bad consequences arising from other psychological tendencies. The curious are also provided with much fun and wisdom long after formal education has ended.

SEVEN:
Kantian Fairness Tendency

Kant was famous for his "categorical imperative," a sort of a "golden rule" that required humans to follow those behavior patterns that, if followed by all others, would make the surrounding human system work best for everybody. And it is not too much to say that modern acculturated man displays, and expects from others, a lot of fairness as thus defined by Kant.

In a small community having a one-way bridge or tunnel for autos, it is the norm in the United States to see a lot of reciprocal courtesy, despite the absence of signs or signals. And many freeway drivers, including myself, will often let other drivers come in front of them, in lane changes or the like, because that is the courtesy they desire when roles are reversed. Moreover, there is, in modern human culture, a lot of courteous lining up by strangers so that all are served on a "first-come-first-served" basis.

Also, strangers often voluntarily share equally in unexpected, unearned good and bad fortune. And, as an obverse consequence of such "fair-sharing" conduct, much reactive hostility occurs when fair-sharing is expected yet not provided.

It is interesting how the world's slavery was pretty well abolished during the last three centuries after being tolerated for a great many previous centuries during which it coexisted with the world's major religions. My guess is that Kantian Fairness Tendency was a major contributor to this result.

EIGHT:
Envy/Jealousy Tendency

A member of a species designed through evolutionary process to want often-scarce food is going to be driven strongly toward getting food when it first sees food. And this is going to occur often and tend to create some conflict when the food is seen in the possession of another member of the same species. This is probably the evolutionary origin of the envy/jealousy Tendency that lies so deep in human nature.

Sibling jealousy is clearly very strong and usually greater in children than adults. It is often stronger than jealousy directed at strangers. Kantian Fairness Tendency probably contributes to this result.

Envy/jealousy is extreme in myth, religion, and literature wherein, in account after account, it triggers hatred and injury. It was regarded as so pernicious by the Jews of the civilization that preceded Christ that it was forbidden, by phrase after phrase, in the laws of Moses. You were even warned by the Prophet not to covet your neighbor's donkey.

And envy/jealousy is also extreme in modern life. For instance, university communities often go bananas when some university employee in money management, or some professor in surgery, gets annual compensation in multiples of the standard professorial salary. And in modern investment banks, law firms, etc., the envy/jealousy effects are usually more extreme than they are in university faculties. Many big law firms, fearing disorder from envy/jealousy, have long treated all senior partners alike in compensation, no matter how different their contributions to firm welfare. As I have shared the observation of life with Warren Buffett over decades, I have heard him wisely say on several occasions: "It is not greed that drives the world, but envy."

And, because this is roughly right, one would expect a vast coverage of envy/jealousy in psychology textbooks. But no such vast coverage existed when I read my three textbooks. Indeed, the very words "envy" and "jealousy" were often absent from indexes.

Nondiscussion of envy/jealousy is not a phenomenon confined to psychology texts. When did any of you last engage in any large group discussion of some issue wherein adult envy/jealousy was identified as the cause of someone's argument? There seems to be a general taboo against any such claim. If so, what accounts for the taboo?

My guess is that people widely and generally sense that labeling some position as driven by envy/jealousy will be regarded as extremely insulting to the position taker, possibly more so when the diagnosis is correct than when it is wrong. And if calling a position "envy-driven" is perceived as the equivalent of describing its holder as a childish mental basket case, then it is quite understandable how a general taboo has arisen.

But should this general taboo extend to psychology texts when it creates such a large gap in the correct, psychological explanation of what is widespread and important? My answer is no.

NINE:
Reciprocation Tendency

The automatic tendency of humans to reciprocate both favors and disfavors has long been noticed as extreme, as it is in apes, monkeys, dogs, and many less cognitively gifted animals. The tendency clearly facilitates group cooperation for the benefit of members. In this respect, it mimics much genetic programming of the social insects.

We see the extreme power of the tendency to reciprocate disfavors in some wars, wherein it increases hatred to a level causing very brutal conduct. For long stretches in many wars, no prisoners were taken; the only acceptable enemy being a dead one. And sometimes that was not enough, as in the case of Genghis Khan, who was not satisfied with corpses. He insisted on their being hacked into pieces.

One interesting mental exercise is to compare Genghis Khan, who exercised extreme, lethal hostility toward other men, with ants that display extreme, lethal hostility toward members of their own species that are not part of their breeding colony. Genghis looks sweetly lovable when compared to the ants. The ants are more disposed to fight and fight with more extreme cruelty. Indeed, E. O. Wilson once waggishly suggested that if ants were suddenly to get atom bombs, all ants would be dead within eighteen hours. What both human and ant history suggest is (1) that nature has no general algorithm making intraspecies, turn-the-other-cheek behavior a booster of species survival, (2) that it is not clear that a country would have good prospects were it to abandon all reciprocate-disfavor tendency directed at outsiders, and (3) if turn-the-other-cheek behavior is a good idea for a country as it deals with outsiders, man's culture is going to have to do a lot of heavy lifting because his genes won't be of much help.

I next turn to man's reciprocated hostility that falls well short of war. Peacetime hostility can be pretty extreme, as in many modern cases of "road rage" or injury-producing temper tantrums on athletic fields.

The standard antidote to one's overactive hostility is to train oneself to defer reaction. As my smart friend Tom Murphy so frequently says, "You can always tell the man off tomorrow, if it is such a good idea."

Of course, the tendency to reciprocate favor for favor is also very intense, so much so that it occasionally reverses the course of reciprocated hostility. Weird pauses in fighting have sometimes occurred right in the middle of wars, triggered by some minor courtesy or favor on the part of one side, followed by favor reciprocation from the other side, and so on, until fighting stopped for a considerable period. This happened more than once in the trench warfare of World War I, over big stretches of the front and much to the dismay of the generals.

It is obvious that commercial trade, a fundamental cause of modern prosperity, is enormously facilitated by man's innate tendency to reciprocate favors. In trade, enlightened self-interest joining with Reciprocation Tendency results in constructive conduct. Daily interchange in marriage is also assisted by Reciprocation Tendency, without which marriage would lose much of its allure.

And Reciprocation Tendency, insomuch as it causes good results, does not join forces only with the superpower of incentives. It also joins Inconsistency-Avoidance Tendency in helping cause (1) the fulfillment of promises made as part of a bargain, including loyalty promises in marriage ceremonies, and (2) correct behavior expected from persons serving as priests, shoemakers, physicians, and all else.

Like other psychological tendencies, and also man's ability to turn somersaults, reciprocate-favor tendency operates to a very considerable degree at a subconscious level. This helps make the tendency a strong force that can sometimes be used by some men to mislead others, which happens all the time.

For instance, when an automobile salesman graciously steers you into a comfortable place to sit and gives you a cup of coffee, you are very likely being tricked, by this small courtesy alone, into parting with an extra five hundred dollars. This is far from the most extreme case of sales success that is rooted in a salesman dispensing minor favors. However, in this scenario of buying a car, you are going to be disadvantaged by parting with an extra five hundred dollars of your own money. This potential loss will protect you to some extent.

But suppose you are the purchasing agent of someone else—a rich employer, for instance. Now the minor favor you receive from the salesman is less opposed by the threat of extra cost to you because someone else is paying the extra cost. Under such circumstances, the salesman is often able to maximize his advantage, particularly when government is the purchaser.

Wise employers, therefore, try to oppose reciprocate-favor tendencies of employees engaged in purchasing. The simplest antidote works best: Don't let them accept any favors from vendors. Sam Walton agreed with this idea of absolute prohibition. He wouldn't let purchasing agents accept so much as a hot dog from a vendor. Given the subconscious level at which much Reciprocation Tendency operates, this policy of Walton's was profoundly correct. If I controlled the Defense Department, its policies would mimic Walton's.

In a famous psychology experiment, Cialdini brilliantly demonstrated the power of "compliance practitioners" to mislead people by triggering their subconscious Reciprocation Tendency.

Carrying out this experiment, Cialdini caused his "compliance practitioners" to wander around his campus and ask strangers to supervise a bunch of juvenile delinquents on a trip to a zoo. Because this happened on a campus, one person in six out of a large sample actually agreed to do this. After accumulating this one-in-six statistic, Cialdini changed his procedure. His practitioners next wandered around the campus asking strangers to devote a big chunk of time every week for two years to the supervision of juvenile delinquents. This ridiculous request got him a one hundred percent rejection rate. But the practitioner had a follow-up question: "Will you at least spend one afternoon taking juvenile delinquents to a zoo?" This raised Cialdini's former acceptance rate of 1/6 to 1/2—a tripling.

What Cialdini's "compliance practitioners" had done was make a small concession, which was reciprocated by a small concession from the other side. This subconscious reciprocation of a concession by Cialdini's experimental subjects actually caused a much increased percentage of them to end up irrationally agreeing to go to a zoo with juvenile delinquents. Now, a professor who can invent an experiment like that, which so powerfully demonstrates something so important, deserves much recognition in the wider world, which he indeed got to the credit of many universities that learned a great deal from Cialdini.

Why is Reciprocation Tendency so important? Well, consider the folly of having law students graduate, and go out in the world representing clients in negotiations, not knowing the nature of the subconscious processes of the mind as exhibited in Cialdini's experiment. Yet such folly was prevalent in the law schools of the world for decades, in fact, generations. The correct name for that is educational malpractice. The law schools didn't know, or care to teach, what Sam Walton so well knew.

The importance and power of reciprocate-favor tendency was also demonstrated in Cialdini's explanation of the foolish decision of the attorney general of the United States to authorize the Watergate burglary. There, an aggressive subordinate made some extreme proposal for advancing Republican interests through use of some combination of whores and a gigantic yacht. When this ridiculous request was rejected, the subordinate backed off, in gracious concession, to merely asking for consent to a burglary, and the attorney general went along. Cialdini believes that subconscious Reciprocation Tendency thus became one important cause of the resignation of a United States president in the Watergate debacle, and so do I. Reciprocation Tendency subtly causes many extreme and dangerous consequences, not just on rare occasions but pretty much all the time.

Man's belief in reciprocate-favor tendency, following eons of his practicing it, has done some queer and bad things in religions. The ritualized murder of the Phoenicians and the Aztecs, in which they sacrificed human victims to their gods, was a particularly egregious example. And we should not forget that as late as the Punic Wars, the civilized Romans, out of fear of defeat, returned in a few instances to the practice of human sacrifice. On the other hand, the reciprocity-based, religion-boosting idea of obtaining help from God in reciprocation for good human behavior has probably been vastly constructive.

Overall, both inside and outside religions, it seems clear to me that Reciprocation Tendency's constructive contributions to man far outweigh its destructive effects. In cases of psychological tendencies being used to counter or prevent bad results from one or more other psychological tendencies—for instance, in the case of interventions to end chemical dependency—you will usually find Reciprocation Tendency performing strongly on the constructive side.

And the very best part of human life probably lies in relationships of affection wherein parties are more interested in pleasing than being pleased—a not uncommon outcome in display of reciprocate-favor tendency.

Before we leave reciprocate-favor tendency, the final phenomenon we will consider is widespread human misery from feelings of guilt. To the extent the feeling of guilt has an evolutionary base, I believe the most plausible cause is the mental conflict triggered in one direction by reciprocate-favor tendency and in the opposite direction by reward superresponse tendency pushing one to enjoy one hundred percent of some good thing. Of course, human culture has often greatly boosted the genetic tendency to suffer from feelings of guilt. Most especially, religious culture has imposed hard-to-follow ethical and devotional demands on people. There is a charming Irish Catholic priest in my neighborhood who, with rough accuracy, often says, "The old Jews may have invented guilt, but we Catholics perfected it." And if you, like me and this priest, believe that, averaged out, feelings of guilt do more good than harm, you may join in my special gratitude for reciprocate-favor tendency, no matter how unpleasant you find feelings of guilt.

TEN:
Influence-from-Mere-Association Tendency

In the standard conditioned reflexes studied by Skinner and most common in the world, responsive behavior, creating a new habit, is directly triggered by rewards previously bestowed. For instance, a man buys a can of branded shoe polish, has a good experience with it when shining his shoes, and because of this "reward," buys the same shoe polish when he needs another can.

But there is another type of conditioned reflex wherein mere association triggers a response. For instance, consider the case of many men who have been trained by their previous experience in life to believe that when several similar items are presented for purchase, the one with the highest price will have the highest quality. Knowing this, some seller of an ordinary industrial product will often change his product's trade dress and raise its price significantly hoping that quality-seeking buyers will be tricked into becoming purchasers by mere association of his product and its high price. This industrial practice frequently is effective in driving up sales and even more so in driving up profits. For instance, it worked wonderfully with high-priced power tools for a long time. And it would work better yet with high-priced pumps at the bottom of oil wells. With luxury goods, the process works with a special boost because buyers who pay high prices often gain extra status from thus demonstrating both their good taste and their ability to pay.

Even association that appears to be trivial, if carefully planned, can have extreme and peculiar effects on purchasers of products. The target purchaser of shoe polish may like pretty girls. And so he chooses the polish with the pretty girl on the can or the one with the pretty girl in the last ad for shoe polish that he saw.

Advertisers know about the power of mere association. You won't see Coke advertised alongside some account of the death of a child. Instead, Coke ads picture life as happier than reality.

Similarly, it is not from mere chance that military bands play such impressive music. That kind of music, appearing in mere association with military service, helps to attract soldiers and keep them in the army. Most armies have learned to use mere association in this successful way.

However, the most damaging miscalculations from mere association do not ordinarily come from advertisers and music providers.

Some of the most important miscalculations come from what is accidentally associated with one's past success, or one's liking and loving, or one's disliking and hating, which includes a natural hatred for bad news.

To avoid being misled by the mere association of some fact with past success, use this memory clue. Think of Napoleon and Hitler when they invaded Russia after using their armies with much success elsewhere. And there are plenty of mundane examples of results like those of Napoleon and Hitler. For instance, a man foolishly gambles in a casino and yet wins. This unlikely correlation causes him to try the casino again, or again and again, to his horrid detriment. Or a man gets lucky in an odds-against venture headed by an untalented friend. So influenced, he tries again what worked before—with terrible results.

The proper antidotes to being made such a patsy by past success are (1) to carefully examine each past success, looking for accidental, non-causative factors associated with such success that will tend to mislead as one appraises odds implicit in a proposed new undertaking and (2) to look for dangerous aspects of the new undertaking that were not present when past success occurred.

The damage to the mind that can come from liking and loving was once demonstrated by obviously false testimony given by an otherwise very admirable woman, the wife of a party in a jury case. The famous opposing counsel wanted to minimize his attack on such an admirable woman yet destroy the credibility of her testimony. And so, in his closing argument, he came to her testimony last. He then shook his head sadly and said, "What are we to make of such testimony? The answer lies in the old rhyme:

> *'As the husband is,*
> *So the wife is.*
> *She is married to a clown,*
> *And the grossness of his nature*
> *Drags her down.'"*

The jury disbelieved the woman's testimony. They easily recognized the strong misinfluence of love on her cognition. And we now often see even stronger misinfluence from love as tearful mothers, with heartfelt conviction, declare before TV cameras the innocence of their obviously guilty sons.

People disagree about how much blindness should accompany the association called love. In *Poor Richard's Almanack* Franklin counseled: "Keep your eyes wide open before marriage and half shut thereafter." Perhaps this "eyes-half-shut" solution is about right, but I favor a tougher prescription: "See it like it is and love anyway."

Hating and disliking also cause miscalculation triggered by mere association. In business, I commonly see people underappraise both the competency and morals of competitors they dislike. This is a dangerous practice, usually disguised because it occurs on a subconscious basis.

Another common bad effect from the mere association of a person and a hated outcome is displayed in "Persian Messenger Syndrome." Ancient Persians actually killed some messengers whose sole fault was that they brought home truthful bad news, say, of a battle lost. It was actually safer for the messenger to run away and hide, instead of doing his job as a wiser boss would have wanted it done.

And Persian Messenger Syndrome is alive and well in modern life, albeit in less lethal versions. It is actually dangerous in many careers to be a carrier of unwelcome news. Union negotiators and employer representatives often know this, and it leads to many tragedies in labor relations. Sometimes lawyers, knowing their clients will hate them if they recommend an unwelcome but wise settlement, will carry on to disaster. Even in places well known for high cognition, one will sometimes find Persian Messenger Syndrome. For instance, years ago, two major oil companies litigated in a Texas trial court over some ambiguity in an operating agreement covering one of the largest oil reservoirs in the Western hemisphere. My guess is that the cause of the trial was some general counsel's unwillingness to carry bad news to a strong-minded CEO.

CBS, in its late heyday, was famous for occurrence of Persian Messenger Syndrome because Chairman Paley was hostile to people who brought him bad news. The result was that Paley lived in a cocoon of unreality, from which he made one bad deal after another, even exchanging a large share of CBS for a company that had to be liquidated shortly thereafter.

The proper antidote to creating Persian Messenger Syndrome and its bad effects, like those at CBS, is to develop, through exercise of will, a habit of welcoming bad news. At Berkshire, there is a common injunction: "Always tell us the bad news promptly. It is only the good news that can wait." It also helps to be so wise and informed that people fear not telling you bad news because you are so likely to get it elsewhere.

Influence-from-Mere-Association Tendency often has a shocking effect that helps swamp the normal tendency to return favor for favor. Sometimes, when one receives a favor, his condition is unpleasant, due to poverty, sickness, subjugation, or something else. In addition, the favor may trigger an envy-driven dislike for the person who was in so favorable a state that he could easily be a favor giver. Under such circumstances, the favor receiver, prompted partly by mere association of the favor giver with past pain, will not only dislike the man who helped him but also try to injure him. This accounts for a famous response, sometimes dubiously attributed to Henry Ford: "Why does that man hate me so? I never did anything for him." I have a friend, whom I will now call "Glotz," who had an amusing experience in favor-giving. Glotz owned an apartment building that he had bought because he wanted, eventually, to use the land in different development. Pending this outcome, Glotz was very lenient in collecting below-market rents from tenants. When, at last, there was a public hearing on Glotz's proposal to tear down the building, one tenant who was far behind in his rent payments was particularly angry and hostile. He came to the public hearing and said, "This proposal is outrageous. Glotz doesn't need any more money. I know this because I was supported in college by Glotz fellowships."

A final serious clump of bad thinking caused by mere association lies in the common use of classification stereotypes. Because Pete knows that Joe is ninety years old and that most ninety-year-old persons don't think very well, Pete appraises old Joe as a thinking klutz even if old Joe still thinks very well. Or, because Jane is a white-haired woman, and Pete knows no old women good at higher math, Pete appraises Jane as no good at it even if Jane is a whiz. This sort of wrong thinking is both natural and common. Pete's antidote is not to believe that, on average, ninety-year-olds think as well as forty-year-olds or that there are as many females as males among Ph. D.'s in math. Instead, just as he must learn that trend does not always correctly predict destiny, he must learn that the average dimension in some group will not reliably guide him to the dimension of some specific item. Otherwise Pete will make many errors, like that of the fellow who drowned in a river that averaged out only eighteen inches deep.

ELEVEN:
Simple, Pain-Avoiding Psychological Denial

This phenomenon first hit me hard in World War II when the superathlete, superstudent son of a family friend flew off over the Atlantic Ocean and never came back. His mother, who was a very sane woman, then refused to believe he was dead. That's Simple, Pain-Avoiding Psychological Denial. The reality is too painful to bear, so one distorts the facts until they become bearable. We all do that to some extent, often causing terrible problems. The tendency's most extreme outcomes are usually mixed up with love, death, and chemical dependency.

Where denial is used to make dying easier, the conduct meets almost no criticism. Who would begrudge a fellow man such help at such a time? But some people hope to leave life hewing to the iron prescription, "It is not necessary to hope in order to persevere." And there is something admirable in anyone able to do this.

In chemical dependency, wherein morals usually break down horribly, addicted persons tend to believe that they remain in respectable condition, with respectable prospects. They thus display an extremely unrealistic denial of reality as they go deeper and deeper into deterioration. In my youth, Freudian remedies failed utterly in reversing chemical dependency, but nowadays Alcoholics Anonymous routinely achieves a fifty percent cure rate by causing several psychological tendencies to act together to counter addiction. However, the cure process is typically difficult and draining, and a fifty percent success rate implies a fifty percent failure rate. One should stay far away from any conduct at all likely to drift into chemical dependency. Even a small chance of suffering so great a damage should be avoided.

TWELVE:
Excessive Self-Regard Tendency

We all commonly observe the excessive self-regard of man. He mostly misappraises himself on the high side, like the ninety percent of Swedish drivers that judge themselves to be above average. Such misappraisals also apply to a person's major "possessions." One spouse usually overappraises the other spouse. And a man's children are likewise appraised higher by him than they are likely to be in a more objective view. Even man's minor possessions tend to be overappraised. Once owned, they suddenly become worth more to him than he would pay if they were offered for sale to him and he didn't already own them. There is a name in psychology for this overappraise-your-own-possessions phenomenon: the "endowment effect." And all man's decisions are suddenly regarded by him as better than would have been the case just before he made them.

Man's excess of self-regard typically makes him strongly

prefer people like himself. Psychology professors have had much fun demonstrating this effect in "lost-wallet" experiments. Their experiments all show that the finder of a lost wallet containing identity clues will be most likely to return the wallet when the owner most closely resembles the finder. Given this quality in psychological nature, cliquish groups of similar persons will always be a very influential part of human culture, even after we wisely try to dampen the worst effects.

Some of the worst consequences in modern life come when dysfunctional groups of cliquish persons, dominated by Excessive Self-Regard Tendency, select as new members of their organizations persons who are very much like themselves. Thus if the English department at an elite university becomes mentally dysfunctional or the sales department of a brokerage firm slips into routine fraud, the problem will have a natural tendency to get worse and to be quite resistant to change for the better. So also with a police department or prison-guard unit or political group gone sour and countless other places mired in evil and folly, such as the worst of our big-city teachers' unions that harm our children by preventing discharge of ineffective teachers. Therefore, some of the most useful members of our civilization are those who are willing to "clean house" when they find a mess under their ambit of control.

Well, naturally, all forms of excess of self-regard cause much error. How could it be otherwise?

Let us consider some foolish gambling decisions. In lotteries, the play is much lower when numbers are distributed randomly than it is when the player picks his own number. This is quite irrational. The odds are almost exactly the same and much against the player. Because state lotteries take advantage of man's irrational love of self-picked numbers, modern man buys more lottery tickets than he otherwise would have, with each purchase foolish.

Intensify man's love of his own conclusions by adding the possessory wallop from the "endowment effect," and you will find that a man who has already bought a pork-belly future on a commodity exchange now foolishly believes, even more strongly than before, in the merits of his speculative bet.

And foolish sports betting, by people who love sports and think they know a lot about relative merits of teams, is a lot more addictive than race track betting—partly because of man's automatic overappraisal of his own complicated conclusions.

Also extremely counterproductive is man's tendency to bet, time after time, in games of skill, like golf or poker, against people who are obviously much better players. Excessive Self-Regard Tendency diminishes the foolish bettor's accuracy in appraising his relative degree of talent.

More counterproductive yet are man's appraisals, typically excessive, of the quality of the future service he is to provide to his business. His overappraisal of these prospective contributions will frequently cause disaster.

Excesses of self-regard often cause bad hiring decisions because employers grossly overappraise the worth of their own conclusions that rely on impressions in face-to-face contact. The correct antidote to this sort of folly is to underweigh face-to-face impressions and overweigh the applicant's past record.

I once chose exactly this course of action while I served as chairman of an academic search committee. I convinced fellow committee members to stop all further interviews and simply appoint a person whose achievement record was much better than that of any other applicant. And when it was suggested to me that I wasn't giving "academic due process," I replied that I was the one being true to academic values because I was using academic research showing poor predictive value of impressions from face-to-face interviews.

Because man is likely to be overinfluenced by face-to-face impressions that by definition involve his active participation, a job candidate who is a marvelous "presenter" often causes great danger under modern executive-search practice. In my opinion, Hewlett-Packard faced just such a danger when it interviewed the articulate, dynamic Carly Fiorina in its search for a new CEO. And I believe (1) that Hewlett-Packard made a bad decision when it chose Ms. Fiorina and (2) that this bad decision would not have been made if Hewlett-Packard had taken the methodological precautions it would have taken if it knew more psychology.

There is a famous passage somewhere in Tolstoy that illuminates the power of Excessive Self-Regard Tendency. According to Tolstoy, the worst criminals don't appraise themselves as all that bad. They come to believe either (1) that they didn't commit their crimes or (2) that, considering the pressures and disadvantages of their lives, it is understandable and forgivable that they behaved as they did and became what they became.

The second half of the "Tolstoy effect", where the man makes excuses for his fixable poor performance, instead of providing the fix, is enormously important. Because a majority of mankind will try to get along by making way too many unreasonable excuses for fixable poor performance, it is very important to have personal and institutional antidotes limiting the ravages of such folly. On the personal level a man should try to face the two simple facts: (1) fixable but unfixed bad performance is bad character and tends to create more of itself, causing more damage to the excuse giver with each tolerated instance, and (2) in demanding places, like athletic teams and General Electric, you are almost sure to be discarded in due course if you keep giving excuses instead of behaving as you should. The main institutional antidotes to this part of the "Tolstoy effect" are (1) a fair, meritocratic, demanding culture plus personnel handling methods that build up morale and (2) severance of the worst offenders. Of course, when you can't sever, as in the case of your own child, you must try to fix the child as best you can. I once heard of a child-teaching method so effective that the child remembered the learning experience over fifty years later. The child later became Dean of the USC School of Music and then related to me what his father said when he saw his child taking candy from the stock of his employer with the excuse that he intended to replace it later. The father said, "Son, it would be better for you to simply take all you want and call yourself a thief every time you do it."

The best antidote to folly from an excess of self-regard is to force yourself to be more objective when you are thinking about yourself, your family and friends, your property, and the value of your past and future activity. This isn't easy to do well and won't work perfectly, but it will work much better than simply letting psychological nature take its normal course.

While an excess of self-regard is often counterproductive in its effects on cognition, it can cause some weird successes from overconfidence that happens to cause success. This factor accounts for the adage: "Never underestimate the man who overestimates himself."

Of course, some high self-appraisals are correct and serve better than false modesty. Moreover, self-regard in the form of a justified pride in a job well done, or a life well lived, is a large constructive force. Without such justified pride, many more airplanes would crash. "Pride" is another word generally left out of psychology textbooks, and this omission is not a good idea. It is also not a good idea to construe the bible's parable about the Pharisee and the Publican as condemning all pride.

Of all forms of useful pride, perhaps the most desirable is a justified pride in being trustworthy. Moreover, the trustworthy man, even after allowing for the inconveniences of his chosen course, ordinarily has a life that averages out better than he would have if he provided less reliability.

THIRTEEN:
Overoptimism Tendency

About three centuries before the birth of Christ, Demosthenes, the most famous Greek orator, said, "What a man wishes, that also will he believe."

Demosthenes, parsed out, was thus saying that man displays not only Simple, Pain-Avoiding Psychological Denial but also an excess of optimism even when he is already doing well.

The Greek orator was clearly right about an excess of optimism being the normal human condition, even when pain or the threat of pain is absent. Witness happy people buying lottery tickets or believing that credit-furnishing, delivery-making grocery stores were going to displace a great many superefficient cash-and-carry supermarkets.

One standard antidote to foolish optimism is trained, habitual use of the simple probability math of Fermat and Pascal, taught in my youth to high school sophomores. The mental rules of thumb that evolution gives you to deal with risk are not adequate. They resemble the dysfunctional golf grip you would have if you relied on a grip driven by evolution instead of golf lessons.

FOURTEEN:
Deprival-Superreaction Tendency

The quantity of man's pleasure from a ten-dollar gain does not exactly match the quantity of his displeasure from a ten-dollar loss. That is, the loss seems to hurt much more than the gain seems to help. Moreover, if a man almost gets something he greatly wants and has it jerked away from him at the last moment, he will react much as if he had long owned the reward and had it jerked away. I include the natural human reactions to both kinds of loss experience—the loss of the possessed reward and the loss of the almost-possessed reward—under one description, Deprival-Superreaction Tendency.

In displaying Deprival-Superreaction Tendency, man frequently incurs disadvantage by misframing his problems. He will often compare what is near instead of what really matters. For instance, a man with $10 million in his brokerage account will often be extremely irritated by the accidental loss of $100 out of the $300 in his wallet.

The Mungers once owned a tame and good-natured dog that displayed the canine version of Deprival-Superreaction Tendency. There was only one way to get bitten by this dog. And that was to try and take some food away from him after he already had it in his mouth. If you did that, this friendly dog would automatically bite. He couldn't help it. Nothing could be more stupid than for the dog to bite his master. But the dog couldn't help being foolish. He had an automatic Deprival-Superreaction Tendency in his nature.

Humans are much the same as this Munger dog. A man ordinarily reacts with irrational intensity to even a small loss, or threatened loss, of property, love, friendship, dominated territory, opportunity, status, or any other valued thing. As a natural result, bureaucratic infighting over the threatened loss of dominated territory often causes immense damage to an institution as a whole. This factor, among others, accounts for much of the wisdom of Jack Welch's long fight against bureaucratic ills at General Electric. Few business leaders have ever conducted wiser campaigns.

Deprival-Superreaction Tendency often protects ideological or religious views by triggering dislike and hatred directed toward vocal nonbelievers. This happens, in part, because the ideas of the nonbelievers, if they spread, will diminish the influence of views that are now supported by a comfortable environment including a strong belief-maintenance system. University liberal arts departments, law schools, and business organizations all display plenty of such ideology-based groupthink that rejects almost all conflicting inputs. When the vocal critic is a former believer, hostility is often boosted both by (1) a concept of betrayal that triggers additional Deprival-Superreaction Tendency because a colleague is lost and (2) fears that conflicting views will have extra persuasive power when they come from a former colleague. The foregoing considerations help account for the old idea of heresy, which for centuries justified much killing of heretics, frequently after torture and frequently accomplished by burning the victim alive.

It is almost everywhere the case that extremes of ideology are maintained with great intensity and with great antipathy to non-believers, causing extremes of cognitive dysfunction. This happens, I believe, because two psychological tendencies are usually acting concurrently toward this same sad result: (1) Inconsistency-Avoidance Tendency, plus (2) Deprival-Superreaction Tendency.

One antidote to intense, deliberate maintenance of groupthink is an extreme culture of courtesy, kept in place despite ideological differences, like the behavior of the justices now serving on the U.S. Supreme Court. Another antidote is to deliberately bring in able and articulate disbelievers of incumbent groupthink. Successful corrective measures to evil examples of groupthink maintenance have included actions like that of Derek Bok when, as president of Harvard, he started disapproving tenure appointments proposed by ideologues at Harvard Law School.

Even a one-degree loss from a 180-degree view will sometime create enough Deprival-Superreaction Tendency to turn a neighbor into an enemy, as I once observed when I bought a house from one of two neighbors locked into hatred by a tiny tree newly installed by one of them.

As the case of these two neighbors illustrated, the clamor of almost any group of neighbors displaying irrational, extreme deprival-superreaction over some trifle in a zoning hearing is not a pretty thing to watch. Such bad behavior drives some people from the zoning field. I once bought some golf clubs from an artisan who was formerly a lawyer. When I asked him what kind of law he had practiced, I expected to hear him say, "divorce law." But his answer was, "zoning law."

Deprival-Superreaction Tendency has ghastly effects in labor relations. Most of the deaths in the labor strife that occurred before World War I came when employers tried to reduce wages. Nowadays, we see fewer deaths and more occasions when whole companies disappear, as competition requires either takeaways from labor—which it will not consent to—or death of the business. Deprival-Superreaction Tendency causes much of this labor resistance, often in cases where it would be in labor's interest to make a different decision.

In contexts other than labor relations, takeaways are also difficult to get. Many tragedies, therefore, occur that would have been avoided had there been more rationality and less subconscious heed of the imperative from Deprival-Superreaction Tendency.

Deprival-Superreaction Tendency is also a huge contributor to ruin from compulsion to gamble. First, it causes the gambler to have a passion to get even once he has suffered loss, and the passion grows with the loss. Second, the most addictive forms of gambling provide a lot of near misses and each one triggers Deprival-Superreaction Tendency. Some slot machine creators are vicious in exploiting this weakness of man. Electronic machines enable these creators to produce a lot of meaningless bar-bar-lemon results that greatly increase play by fools who think they have very nearly won large rewards.

Deprival-Superreaction Tendency often does much damage to man in open-outcry auctions. The "social proof" that we will next consider tends to convince man that the last price from another bidder was reasonable, and then Deprival-Superreaction Tendency prompts him strongly to top the last bid. The best antidote to being thus triggered into paying foolish prices at open-outcry auctions is the simple Buffett practice: Don't go to such auctions.

Deprival-Superreaction Tendency and Inconsistency-Avoidance Tendency often join to cause one form of business failure. In this form of ruin, a man gradually uses up all his good assets in a fruitless attempt to rescue a big venture going bad. One of the best antidotes to this folly is good poker skill learned young. The teaching value of poker demonstrates that not all effective teaching occurs on a standard academic path.

I myself, the would-be instructor here, many decades ago made a big mistake caused in part by subconscious operation of my Deprival-Superreaction Tendency. A friendly broker called and offered me 300 shares of ridiculously underpriced, very thinly traded Belridge Oil at $115 per share, which I purchased using cash I had on hand. The next day, he offered me 1,500 more shares at the same price, which I declined to buy partly because I could only have made the purchase had I sold something or borrowed the required $173,000. This was a very irrational decision. I was a well-to-do man with no debt; there was no risk of loss; and similar no-risk opportunities were not likely to come along. Within two years, Belridge Oil sold out to Shell at a price of about $3,700 per share, which made me about $5.4 million poorer than I would have been had I then been psychologically acute. As this tale demonstrates, psychological ignorance can be very expensive.

Some people may question my defining Deprival-Superreaction Tendency to include reaction to profit barely missed, as in the well-documented responses of slot machine players. However, I believe that I haven't defined the tendency as broadly as I should. My reason for suggesting an even broader definition is that many Berkshire Hathaway shareholders I know never sell or give away a single share after immense gains in market value have occurred. Some of this reaction is caused by rational calculation, and some is, no doubt, attributable to some combination of (1) reward superresponse, (2) "status quo bias" from Inconsistency-Avoidance Tendency, and (3) "the endowment effect" from Excessive Self-Regard Tendency. But I believe the single strongest irrational explanation is a form of Deprival-Superreaction Tendency. Many of these shareholders simply can't stand the idea of having their Berkshire Hathaway holdings smaller. Partly they dislike facing what they consider an impairment of identity, but mostly they fear missing out on future gains from stock sold or given away.

FIFTEEN:
Social-Proof Tendency

The otherwise complex behavior of man is much simplified when he automatically thinks and does what he observes to be thought and done around him. And such followership often works fine. For instance, what simpler way could there be to find out how to walk to a big football game in a strange city than by following the flow of the crowd. For some such reason, man's evolution left him with Social-Proof Tendency, an automatic tendency to think and act as he sees others around him thinking and acting.

Psychology professors love Social-Proof Tendency because in their experiments it causes ridiculous results. For instance, if a professor arranges for some stranger to enter an elevator wherein ten "compliance practitioners" are all silently standing so that they face the rear of the elevator, the stranger will often turn around and do the same. The psychology professors can also use Social-Proof Tendency to cause people to make large and ridiculous measurement errors.

And, of course, teenagers' parents usually learn more than they would like about teenagers' cognitive errors from Social-Proof Tendency. This phenomenon was recently involved in a breakthrough by Judith Rich Harris who demonstrated that superrespect by young people for their peers, rather than for parents or other adults, is ordained to some considerable extent by the genes of the young people. This makes it wise for parents to rely more on manipulating the quality of the peers than on exhortations to their own offspring. A person like Ms. Harris, who can provide an insight of this quality and utility, backed by new reasons, has not lived in vain.

And in the highest reaches of business, it is not all uncommon to find leaders who display followership akin to that of teenagers. If one oil company foolishly buys a mine, other oil companies often quickly join in buying mines. So also if the purchased company makes fertilizer. Both of these oil company buying fads actually bloomed, with bad results.

Of course, it is difficult to identify and correctly weigh all the possible ways to deploy the cash flow of an oil company. So oil company executives, like everyone else, have made many bad decisions that were quickly triggered by discomfort from doubt. Going along with social proof provided by the action of other oil companies ends this discomfort in a natural way.

When will Social-Proof Tendency be most easily triggered? Here the answer is clear from many experiments: Triggering most readily occurs in the presence of puzzlement or stress, and particularly when both exist.

Because stress intensifies Social-Proof Tendency, disreputable sales organizations, engaged, for instance, in such action as selling swampland to schoolteachers, manipulate targets into situations combining isolation and stress. The isolation strengthens the social proof provided by both the knaves and the people who buy first, and the stress, often increased by fatigue, augments the targets' susceptibility to the social proof. And, of course, the techniques of our worst "religious" cults imitate those of the knavish salesmen. One cult even used rattlesnakes to heighten the stress felt by conversion targets.

Because both bad and good behavior are made contagious by Social-Proof Tendency, it is highly important that human societies (1) stop any bad behavior before it spreads and (2) foster and display all good behavior.

My father once told me that just after commencing law practice in Omaha, he went with a large group from Nebraska to South Dakota to hunt pheasants. A South Dakota hunting license was, say, $2 for South Dakota residents and $5 for nonresidents. All the Nebraska residents, one by one, signed up for South Dakota licenses with phony South Dakota addresses until it was my father's turn. Then, according to him, he barely prevented himself from doing what the others were doing, which was some sort of criminal offense.

Not everyone so resists the social contagion of bad behavior. And, therefore, we often get "Serpico Syndrome," named to commemorate the state of a near-totally corrupt New York police division joined by Frank Serpico. He was then nearly murdered by gunfire because of his resistance to going along with the corruption in the division. Such corruption was being driven by social proof plus incentives, the combination that creates Serpico Syndrome. The Serpico story should be taught more than it now is because the didactic power of its horror is aimed at a very important evil, driven substantially by a very important force: social proof.

In social proof, it is not only action by others that misleads but also their inaction. In the presence of doubt, inaction by others becomes social proof that inaction is the right course. Thus, the inaction of a great many bystanders led to the death of Kitty Genovese in a famous incident much discussed in introductory psychology courses.

In the ambit of social proof, the outside directors on a corporate board usually display the near ultimate form of inaction. They fail to object to anything much short of an axe murder until some public embarrassment of the board finally causes their intervention. A typical board-of-directors' culture was once well described by my friend, Joe Rosenfield, as he said, "They asked me if I wanted to become a director of Northwest Bell, and it was the last thing they ever asked me."

In advertising and sales promotion, Social-Proof Tendency is about as strong a factor as one could imagine. "Monkey-see, monkey-do" is the old phrase that reminds one of how strongly John will often wish to do something, or have something, just because Joe does or has it. One interesting consequence is that an advertiser will pay a lot to have its soup can, instead of someone else's, in a movie scene involving soup consumption only in a peripheral way.

Social-Proof Tendency often interacts in a perverse way with Envy/Jealousy and Deprival-Superreaction Tendency. One such interaction amused my family for years as people recalled the time when my cousin Russ and I, at ages three and four, fought and howled over a single surplus shingle while surrounded by a virtual sea of surplus shingles.

But the adult versions of this occasion, boosted by psychological tendencies preserving ideologies, are not funny and can bring down whole civilizations. The Middle East now presents just such a threat. By now the resources spent by Jews, Arabs and all others over a small amount of disputed land if divided arbitrarily among land claimants, would have made every one better off, even before taking into account any benefit from reduced threat of war, possibly nuclear.

Outside domestic relations it is rare now to try to resolve disputes by techniques including discussion of impacts from psychological tendencies. Considering the implications of childishness that would be raised by such inclusion, and the defects of psychology as now taught, this result may be sound. But, given the nuclear stakes now involved and the many failures in important negotiations lasting decades, I often wonder if some day, in some way, more use of psychological insight will eventually improve outcomes. If so, correct teaching of psychology matters a lot. And, if old psychology professors are even less likely than old physics professors to learn new ways, which seems nearly certain, then we may, as Max Planck predicted, need a new generation of psychology professors who have grown up to think in a different way.

If only one lesson is to be chosen from a package of lessons involving Social-Proof Tendency, and used in self improvement, my favorite would be: Learn how to ignore the examples from others when they are wrong, because few skills are more worth having.

SIXTEEN:
Contrast-Misreaction Tendency

Because the nervous system of man does not naturally measure in absolute scientific units, it must instead rely on something simpler. The eyes have a solution that limits their programming needs: the contrast in what is seen is registered. And as in sight, so does it go, largely, in the other senses. Moreover, as perception goes, so goes cognition. The result is man's Contrast-Misreaction Tendency.

Few psychological tendencies do more damage to correct thinking. Small-scale damages involve instances such as man's buying an overpriced $1,000 leather dashboard merely because the price is so low compared to his concurrent purchase of a $65,000 car. Large-scale damages often ruin lives, as when a wonderful woman having terrible parents marries a man who would be judged satisfactory only in comparison to her parents. Or as when a man takes wife number two who would be appraised as all right only in comparison to wife number one.

A particularly reprehensible form of sales practice occurs in the offices of some real estate brokers. A buyer from out of the city, perhaps needing to shift his family there, visits the office with little time available. The salesman deliberately shows the customer three awful houses at ridiculously high prices. Then he shows him a merely bad house at a price only moderately too high. And, boom, the broker often makes an easy sale.

Contrast-Misreaction Tendency is routinely used to cause disadvantage for customers buying merchandise and services. To make an ordinary price seem low, the vendor will very frequently create a highly artificial price that is much higher than the price always sought, then advertise his standard price as a big reduction from his phony price. Even when people know that this sort of customer manipulation is being attempted, it will often work to trigger buying. This phenomenon accounts in part for much advertising in newspapers. It also demonstrates that being aware of psychological ploys is not a perfect defense.

When a man's steps are consecutively taken toward disaster, with each step being very small, the brain's Contrast-Misreaction Tendency will often let the man go too far toward disaster to be able to avoid it. This happens because each step presents so small a contrast from his present position.

A bridge-playing pal of mine once told me that a frog tossed into very hot water would jump out, but that the same frog would end up dying if placed in room-temperature water that was later heated at a very slow rate. My few shreds of physiological knowledge make me doubt this account. But no matter because many businesses die in just the manner claimed by my friend for the frog. Cognition, misled by tiny changes involving low contrast, will often miss a trend that is destiny.

One of Ben Franklin's best-remembered and most useful aphorisms is "A small leak will sink a great ship." The utility of the aphorism is large precisely because the brain so often misses the functional equivalent of a small leak in a great ship.

SEVENTEEN:
Stress-Influence Tendency

Everyone recognizes that sudden stress, for instance from a threat, will cause a rush of adrenaline in the human body, prompting faster and more extreme reaction. And everyone who has taken Psych 101 knows that stress makes Social-Proof Tendency more powerful.

In a phenomenon less well recognized but still widely known, light stress can slightly improve performance—say, in examinations—whereas heavy stress causes dysfunction.

But few people know more about really heavy stress than that it can cause depression. For instance, most people know that an "acute stress depression" makes thinking dysfunctional because it causes an extreme of pessimism, often extended in length and usually accompanied by activity-stopping fatigue. Fortunately, as most people also know, such a depression is one of mankind's more reversible ailments. Even before modern drugs were available, many people afflicted by depression, such as Winston Churchill and Samuel Johnson, gained great achievement in life.

Most people know very little about nondepressive mental breakdowns influenced by heavy stress. But there is at least one exception, involving the work of Pavlov when he was in his seventies and eighties. Pavlov had won a Nobel Prize early in life by using dogs to work out the physiology of digestion. Then he became world-famous by working out mere-association responses in dogs, initially salivating dogs—so much so that changes in behavior triggered by mere-association, like those caused by much modern advertisement, are today often said to come from "Pavlovian" conditioning.

What happened to cause Pavlov's last work was especially interesting. During the great Leningrad Flood of the 1920s, Pavlov had many dogs in cages. Their habits had been transformed, by a combination of his "Pavlovian conditioning" plus standard reward responses, into distinct and different patterns. As the waters of the flood came up and receded, many dogs reached a point where they had almost no airspace between their noses and the tops of their cages. This subjected them to maximum stress. Immediately thereafter, Pavlov noticed that many of the dogs were no longer behaving as they had. The dog that formerly had liked his trainer now disliked him, for example. This result reminds one of modern cognition reversals in which a person's love of his parents suddenly becomes hate, as new love has been shifted suddenly to a cult. The unanticipated, extreme changes in Pavlov's dogs would have driven any good experimental scientist into a near-frenzy of curiosity. That was indeed Pavlov's reaction. But not many scientists would have done what Pavlov next did.

And that was to spend the rest of his long life giving stress-induced nervous breakdowns to dogs, after which he would try to reverse the breakdowns, all the while keeping careful experimental records. He found (1) that he could classify dogs so as to predict how easily a particular dog would breakdown; (2) that the dogs hardest to break down were also the hardest to return to their pre-breakdown state; (3) that any dog could be broken down; and (4) that he couldn't reverse a breakdown except by reimposing stress.

Now, practically everyone is revolted by such experimental treatment of man's friend, the dog. Moreover, Pavlov was Russian and did his last work under the Communists. And maybe those facts account for the present extreme, widespread ignorance of Pavlov's last work. The two Freudian psychiatrists with whom I tried many years ago to discuss this work had never heard of it. And the dean of a major medical school actually asked me, several years ago, if any of Pavlov's experiments were "repeatable" in experiments of other researchers. Obviously, Pavlov is now a sort of forgotten hero in medical science.

I first found a description of Pavlov's last work in a popular paperback, written by some Rockefeller-financed psychiatrist, when I was trying to figure out (1) how cults worked their horrible mischief and (2) what should the law say about what parents could do to "deprogram" children who had become brainwashed zombies. Naturally, mainstream law objected to the zombies being physically captured by their parents and next subjected to stress that would help to deprogram the effects of the stress they had endured in cult conversions.

I never wanted to get into the legal controversy that existed about this subject. But I did conclude that the controversy couldn't be handled with maximized rationality without considering whether, as Pavlov's last work suggests, the heavy-handed imposition of stress might be the only reversal method that would work to remedy one of the worst evils imaginable: a stolen mind. I have included this discussion of Pavlov (1) partly out of general antagonism toward taboos, (2) partly to make my talk reasonably complete as it considers stress and (3) partly because I hope some listener may continue my inquiry with more success.

EIGHTEEN:
Availability-Misweighing Tendency

This mental tendency echoes the words of the song: "When I'm not near the girl I love, I love the girl I'm near." Man's imperfect, limited-capacity brain easily drifts into working with what's easily available to it. And the brain can't use what it can't remember or what it is blocked from recognizing because it is heavily influenced by one or more psychological tendencies bearing strongly on it, as the fellow is influenced by the nearby girl in the song. And so the mind overweighs what is easily available and thus displays Availability-Misweighing Tendency.

The main antidote to miscues from Availability-Misweighing Tendency often involve procedures, including use of checklists, which are almost always helpful.

Another antidote is to behave somewhat like Darwin did when he emphasized disconfirming evidence. What should be done is to especially emphasize factors that don't produce reams of easily available numbers, instead of drifting mostly or entirely into considering factors that do produce such numbers. Still another antidote is to find and hire some skeptical, articulate people with far-reaching minds to act as advocates for notions that are opposite to the incumbent notions.

One consequence of this tendency is that extra-vivid evidence, being so memorable and thus more available in cognition, should often consciously be underweighed while less vivid evidence should be overweighed.

Still, the special strength of extra-vivid images in influencing the mind can be constructively used (1) in persuading someone else to reach a correct conclusion or (2) as a device for improving one's own memory by attaching vivid images, one after the other, to many items one doesn't want to forget. Indeed, such use of vivid images as memory boosters is what enabled the great orators of classical Greece and Rome to give such long, organized speeches without using notes.

The great algorithm to remember in dealing with this tendency is simple: An idea or a fact is not worth more merely because it is easily available to you.

NINETEEN:
Use-It-or-Lose-It Tendency

All skills attenuate with disuse. I was a whiz at calculus until age twenty, after which the skill was soon obliterated by total nonuse. The right antidote to such a loss is to make use of the functional equivalent of the aircraft simulator employed in pilot training. This allows a pilot to continuously practice all of the rarely used skills that he can't afford to lose.

Throughout his life, a wise man engages in practice of all his useful, rarely used skills, many of them outside his discipline, as a sort of duty to his better self. If he reduces the number of skills he practices and, therefore, the number of skills he retains, he will naturally drift into error from man with a hammer tendency.

His learning capacity will also shrink as he creates gaps in the latticework of theory he needs as a framework for understanding new experience.

It is also essential for a thinking man to assemble his skills into a checklist that he routinely uses. Any other mode of operation will cause him to miss much that is important.

Skills of a very high order can be maintained only with daily practice. The pianist Paderewski once said that if he failed to practice for a single day, he could notice his performance deterioration and that, after a week's gap in practice, the audience could notice it as well.

The hard rule of Use-It-or-Lose-It Tendency tempers its harshness for the diligent. If a skill is raised to fluency, instead of merely being crammed in briefly to enable one to pass some test, then the skill (1) will be lost more slowly and (2) will come back faster when refreshed with new learning. These are not minor advantages, and a wise man engaged in learning some important skill will not stop until he is really fluent in it.

TWENTY:
Drug-Misinfluence Tendency

This tendency's destructive power is so widely known to be intense, with frequent tragic consequences for cognition and the outcome of life, that it needs no discussion here to supplement that previously given under "Simple, Pain-Avoiding Psychological Denial."

TWENTY-ONE:
Senescence-Misinfluence Tendency

With advanced age, there comes a natural cognitive decay, differing among individuals in the earliness of its arrival and the speed of its progression. Practically no one is good at learning complex new skills when very old. But some people remain pretty good in maintaining intensely practiced old skills until late in life, as one can notice in many a bridge tournament.

Old people like me get pretty skilled, without working at it, at disguising age-related deterioration because social convention, like clothing, hides much decline.

Continuous thinking and learning, done with joy, can somewhat help delay what is inevitable.

TWENTY-TWO:
Authority-Misinfluence Tendency

Living in dominance hierarchies as he does, like all his ancestors before him, man was born mostly to follow leaders, with only a few people doing the leading. And so, human society is formally organized into dominance hierarchies, with their culture augmenting the natural follow-the-leader tendency of man.

But automatic as most human reactions are, with the tendency to follow leaders being no exception, man is often destined to suffer greatly when the leader is wrong or when his leader's ideas don't get through properly in the bustle of life and are misunderstood. And so, we find much miscognition from man's Authority-Misinfluence Tendency.

Some of the misinfluences are amusing, as in a case described by Cialdini. A physician left a written order for a nurse treating an earache, as follows: "Two drops, twice a day, 'r. ear.'" The nurse then directed the patient to turn over and put the eardrops in his anus.

Other versions of confused instructions from authority figures are tragic. In World War II, a new pilot for a general, who sat beside him in the copilot's seat, was so anxious to please his boss that he misinterpreted some minor shift in the general's position as a direction to do some foolish thing. The pilot crashed the plane and became a paraplegic.

Well, naturally, cases like this one get the attention of careful thinkers like Boss Buffett, who always acts like an overquiet mouse around his pilots.

Such cases are also given attention in the simulator training of copilots who have to learn to ignore certain really foolish orders from boss pilots because boss pilots will sometimes err disastrously. Even after going through such a training regime, however, copilots in simulator exercises will too often allow the simulated plane to crash because of some extreme and perfectly obvious simulated error of the chief pilot.

After Corporal Hitler had risen to dominate Germany, leading a bunch of believing Lutherans and Catholics into orgies of genocide and other mass destruction, one clever psychology professor, Stanley Milgram, decided to do an experiment to determine exactly how far authority figures could lead ordinary people into gross misbehavior. In this experiment, a man posing as an authority figure, namely a professor governing a respectable experiment, was able to trick a great many ordinary people into giving what they had every reason to believe were massive electric shocks that inflicted heavy torture on innocent fellow citizens. This experiment did demonstrate a terrible result contributed to by Authority-Misinfluence Tendency, but it also demonstrated extreme ignorance in the psychology professoriate right after World War II.

Almost any intelligent person with my checklist of psychological tendencies in his hand would, by simply going down the checklist, have seen that Milgram's experiment involved about six powerful psychological tendencies acting in confluence to bring about his extreme experimental result. For instance, the person pushing Milgram's shock lever was given much social proof from presence of inactive bystanders whose silence communicated that his behavior was okay. Yet it took over a thousand psychological papers, published before I got to Milgram, for the professoriate to get his experiment only about ninety percent as well understood as it would have immediately been by any intelligent person who used (1) any sensible organization of psychology along the lines of this talk, plus (2) a checklist procedure. This outcome displaying the dysfunctional thinking of long-dead professors deserves a better explanation. I will later deal with the subject in a very hesitant fashion.

We can be pleased that the psychology professoriate of a former era wasn't quite as dysfunctional as the angler in my next-to-last illustration of Authority-Misinfluence Tendency.

When I once fished in the Rio Colorado in Costa Rica, my guide, in a state of shock, told me a story about an angler who'd earlier come to the river without ever having fished for tarpon. A fishing guide like the one I had runs the boat and gives fishing advice, establishing himself in this context as the ultimate authority figure. In the case of this guide, his native language was Spanish, while the angler's native language was English. The angler got a big tarpon on and began submitting to many directions from this authority figure called a guide: tip up, tip down, reel in, etc. Finally, when it was necessary to put more pressure on the fish by causing more bending of the angler's rod, the guide said in English: "Give him the rod, give him the rod." Well, the angler threw his expensive rod at the fish, and when last seen, it was going down the Rio Colorado toward the ocean. This example shows how powerful is the tendency to go along with an authority figure and how it can turn one's brain into mush.

My final example comes from business. A psychology Ph. D. once became a CEO of a major company and went wild, creating an expensive new headquarters, with a great wine cellar, at an isolated site. At some point, his underlings remonstrated that money was running short. "Take the money out of the depreciation reserves," said the CEO. Not too easy because a depreciation reserve is a liability account.

So strong is undue respect for authority that this CEO, and many even worse examples, have actually been allowed to remain in control of important business institutions for long periods after it was clear they should be removed. The obvious implication: Be careful whom you appoint to power because a dominant authority figure will often be hard to remove, aided as he will be by Authority-Misinfluence Tendency.

TWENTY-THREE:
Twaddle Tendency

Man, as a social animal who has the gift of language, is born to prattle and to pour out twaddle that does much damage when serious work is being attempted. Some people produce copious amounts of twaddle and others very little.

A trouble from the honeybee version of twaddle was once demonstrated in an interesting experiment. A honeybee normally goes out and finds nectar and then comes back and does a dance that communicates to the other bees where the nectar is. The other bees then go out and get it. Well some scientist—clever, like B. F. Skinner—decided to see how well a honeybee would do with a handicap. He put the nectar straight up. Way up. Well, in a natural setting, there is no nectar a long way straight up, and the poor honeybee doesn't have a genetic program that is adequate to handle what she now has to communicate. You might guess that this honeybee would come back to the hive and slink into a corner, but she doesn't. She comes into the hive and does an incoherent dance. Well, all my life I've been dealing with the human equivalent of that honeybee. And it's a very important part of wise administration to keep prattling people, pouring out twaddle, far away from the serious work. A rightly famous Caltech engineering professor, exhibiting more insight than tact, once expressed his version of this idea as follows: "The principal job of an academic administration is to keep the people who don't matter from interfering with the work of the people that do." I include this quotation partly because I long suffered from backlash caused by my version of this professor's conversational manner. After much effort, I was able to improve only slightly, so one of my reasons for supplying the quotation is my hope that, at least in comparison, I will appear tactful.

TWENTY-FOUR:
Reason-Respecting Tendency

There is in man, particularly one in an advanced culture, a natural love of accurate cognition and a joy in its exercise. This accounts for the widespread popularity of crossword puzzles, other puzzles, and bridge and chess columns, as well as all games requiring mental skill.

This tendency has an obvious implication. It makes man especially prone to learn well when a would-be teacher gives correct reasons for what is taught, instead of simply laying out the desired belief ex cathedra with no reasons given. Few practices, therefore, are wiser than not only thinking through reasons before giving orders but also communicating these reasons to the recipient of the order.

No one knew this better than Carl Braun, who designed oil refineries with spectacular skill and integrity. He had a very simple rule, one of many in his large, Teutonic company: You had to tell Who was to do What, Where, When, and Why. And if you wrote a communication leaving out your explanation of why the addressee was to do what was ordered, Braun was likely to fire you because Braun well knew that ideas got through best when reasons for the ideas were meticulously laid out.

In general, learning is most easily assimilated and used when, life long, people consistently hang their experience, actual and vicarious, on a latticework of theory answering the question: Why? Indeed, the question "Why?" is a sort of Rosetta stone opening up the major potentiality of mental life.

Unfortunately, Reason-Respecting Tendency is so strong that even a person's giving of meaningless or incorrect reasons will increase compliance with his orders and requests. This has been demonstrated in psychology experiments wherein "compliance practitioners" successfully jump to the head of the lines in front of copying machines by explaining their reason: "I have to make some copies." This sort of unfortunate byproduct of Reason-Respecting Tendency is a conditioned reflex, based on a widespread appreciation of the importance of reasons. And, naturally, the practice of laying out various claptrap reasons is much used by commercial and cult "compliance practitioners" to help them get what they don't deserve.

TWENTY-FIVE:
Lollapalooza Tendency—The Tendency to Get Extreme Consequences from Confluences of Psychological Tendencies Acting in Favor of a Particular Outcome

This tendency was not in any of the psychology texts I once examined, at least in any coherent fashion, yet it dominates life. It accounts for the extreme result in the Milgram experiment and the extreme success of some cults that have stumbled through practice evolution into bringing pressure from many psychological tendencies to bear at the same time on conversion targets. The targets vary in susceptibility, like the dogs Pavlov worked with in his old age, but some of the minds that are targeted simply snap into zombiedom under cult pressure. Indeed, that is one cult's name for the conversion phenomenon: snapping.

What are we to make of the extreme ignorance of the psychology textbook writers of yesteryear? How could anyone who had taken a freshman course in physics or chemistry not be driven to consider, above all, how psychological tendencies combine and with what effects? Why would anyone think his study of psychology was adequate without his having endured the complexity involved in dealing with intertwined psychological tendencies? What could be more ironic than professors using oversimplified notions while studying bad cognitive effects grounded in the mind's tendency to use oversimplified algorithms?

I will make a few tentative suggestions. Maybe many of the long-dead professors wanted to create a whole science from one narrow type of repeatable psychology experiment that was conductible in a university setting and that aimed at one psychological tendency at a time. If so, these early psychology professors made a massive error in so restricting their approach to their subject. It would be like physics ignoring (1) astrophysics because it couldn't happen in a physics lab, plus (2) all compound effects. What psychological tendencies could account for early psychology professors adopting an over-restricted approach to their own subject matter? One candidate would be Availability-Misweighing Tendency grounded in a preference for easy-to-control data. And then the restrictions would eventually create an extreme case of man with a hammer tendency. Another candidate might be envy/jealousy Tendency through which early psychology professors displayed some weird form of envy of a physics that was misunderstood. And this possibility tends to demonstrate that leaving envy/jealousy out of academic psychology was never a good idea.

I now quitclaim all these historical mysteries to my betters.

Well, that ends my brief description of psychological tendencies.

QUESTIONS AND ANSWERS:

Now, as promised, I will ask and answer a few general questions.

My first is a compound question: Isn't this list of psychological tendencies tautological to some extent compared to the system of Euclid? That is, aren't there overlaps in the tendencies? And couldn't the system be laid out just as plausibly in a somewhat different way? The answers are yes, yes, and yes, but this matters only moderately. Further refinement of these tendencies, while desirable, has a limited practical potential because a significant amount of messiness is unfixable in a soft science like psychology.

My second question is: Can you supply a real-world model, instead of a Milgram-type controlled psychology experiment, that uses your system to illustrate multiple psychological tendencies interacting in a plausibly diagnosable way? The answer is yes. One of my favorite cases involves the McDonnell Douglas airliner evacuation test. Before a new airliner can be sold, the government requires that it pass an evacuation test, during which a full load of passengers must get out in some short period of time. The government directs that the test be realistic. So you can't pass by evacuating only twenty-year-old athletes. So McDonnell Douglas scheduled such a test in a darkened hangar using a lot of old people as evacuees. The passenger cabin was, say, twenty feet above the concrete floor of the hangar and was to be evacuated through moderately flimsy rubber chutes. The first test was made in the morning. There were about twenty very serious injuries, and the evacuation took so long it flunked the time test. So what did McDonnell Douglas next do? It repeated the test in the afternoon, and this time there was another failure, with about twenty more serious injuries, including one case of permanent paralysis.

What psychological tendencies contributed to this terrible result? Well, using my tendency list as a checklist, I come up with the following explanation. Reward-Superresponse Tendency drove McDonnell Douglas to act fast. It couldn't sell its airliner until it passed the test. Also pushing the company was Doubt-Avoidance Tendency with its natural drive to arrive at a decision and run with it. Then the government's direction that the test be realistic drove Authority-Misinfluence Tendency into the mischief of causing McDonnell Douglas to overreact by using what was obviously too dangerous a test method. By now the course of action had been decided, so Inconsistency-Avoidance Tendency helped preserve the near-idiotic plan. When all the old people got to the dark hangar, with its high airline cabin and concrete floor, the situation must have made McDonnell Douglas employees very queasy, but they saw other employees and supervisors not objecting. Social-Proof Tendency, therefore, swamped the queasiness. And this allowed continued action as planned, a continuation that was aided by more Authority-Misinfluence Tendency.

Then came the disaster of the morning test with its failure, plus serious injuries. McDonnell Douglas ignored the strong disconfirming evidence from the failure of the first test because confirmation bias, aided by the triggering of strong Deprival-Superreaction Tendency, favored maintaining the original plan. McDonnell Douglas' Deprival-Superreaction Tendency was now like that which causes a gambler, bent on getting even after a huge loss, to make his final big bet. After all, McDonnell Douglas was going to lose a lot if it didn't pass its test as scheduled. More psychology-based explanation can probably be made, but the foregoing discussion is complete enough to demonstrate the utility of my system when used in a checklist mode.

My third question is also compound: In the practical world, what good is the thought system laid out in this list of tendencies? Isn't practical benefit prevented because these psychological tendencies are so thoroughly programmed into the human mind by broad evolution [the combination of genetic and cultural evolution] that we can't get rid of them? Well, the answer is that the tendencies are probably much more good than bad. Otherwise, they wouldn't be there, working pretty well for man, given his condition and his limited brain capacity. So the tendencies can't be simply washed out automatically, and shouldn't be. Nevertheless, the psychological thought system described, when properly understood and used, enables the spread of wisdom and good conduct and facilitates the avoidance of disaster. Tendency is not always destiny, and knowing the tendencies and their antidotes can often help prevent trouble that would otherwise occur. Here is a short list of examples reminding us of the great utility of elementary psychological knowledge:

One: Carl Braun's communication practices.

Two: The use of simulators in pilot training.

Three: The system of Alcoholics Anonymous.

Four: Clinical training methods in medical schools.

Five: The rules of the U.S. Constitutional Convention: totally secret meetings, no recorded vote by name until the final vote, votes reversible at any time before the end of the convention, then just one vote on the whole Constitution. These are very clever psychology-respecting rules. If the founders had used a different procedure, many people would have been pushed by various psychological tendencies into inconsistent, hardened positions. The elite founders got our Constitution through by a whisker only because they were psychologically acute.

Six: *The use of Granny's incentive-driven rule to manipulate oneself toward better performance of one's duties.*

Seven: *The Harvard Business School's emphasis on decision trees. When I was young and foolish I used to laugh at the Harvard Business School. I said, "They're teaching twenty-eight-year-old people that high school algebra works in real life?" But later, I wised up and realized that it was very important that they do that to counter some bad effects from psychological tendencies. Better late than never.*

Eight: *The use of autopsy equivalents at Johnson & Johnson. At most corporations, if you make an acquisition and it turns out to be a disaster, all the people, paperwork, and presentations that caused the foolish acquisition are quickly forgotten. Nobody wants to be associated with the poor outcome by mentioning it. But at Johnson & Johnson, the rules make everybody revisit old acquisitions, comparing predictions with outcomes. That is a very smart thing to do.*

Nine: *The great example of Charles Darwin as he avoided confirmation bias, which has morphed into the extreme anti-confirmation-bias method of the "double blind" studies wisely required in drug research by the F.D.A.*

Ten: *The Warren Buffett rule for open-outcry auctions: Don't go.*

My fourth question is: What special knowledge problems lie buried in the thought system demonstrated by your list?

Well, one answer is paradox. In social psychology, the more people learn about the system the less it is true, and this is what gives the system its great value as a preventer of bad outcomes and a driver of good outcomes. This result is paradoxical, and doesn't remind one of elementary physics, but so what. One can't get all the paradox out of pure math, so why should psychology be shocked by some paradox?

There is also some paradox in cognition change that works even when the manipulated person knows he is being manipulated. This creates a sort of paradox in a paradox, but, again, so what. I once much enjoyed an occasion of this sort. I drew this beautiful woman as my dinner partner many years ago. I'd never seen her before. She was married to a prominent Los Angeles man. She sat down next to me, turned her beautiful face up, and said, "Charlie, what one word accounts for your remarkable success in life?" I knew I was being manipulated by a practiced routine, and I just loved it. I never see this woman without a little lift in my spirits. And, by the way, I told her I was rational. You'll have to judge yourself whether that's true. I may be demonstrating some psychological tendency I hadn't planned on demonstrating.

My fifth question is: Don't we need more reconciliation of psychology and economics? My answer is yes, and I suspect that some slight progress is being made. I have heard of one such example. Colin Camerer of Caltech, who works in "experimental economics," devised an interesting experiment in which he caused high I.Q. students, playing for real money, to pay price A+B for a "security" they knew would turn into A dollars at the end of the day. This foolish action occurred because the students were allowed to trade with each other in a liquid market for the security. And some students then paid price A+B because they hoped to unload on other students at a higher price before the day was over.

What I will now confidently predict is that, despite Camerer's experimental outcome, most economics and corporate finance professors who still believe in the "hard-form efficient market hypothesis" will retain their original belief. If so, this will be one more indication of how irrational smart people can be when influenced by psychological tendencies.

My sixth question is: Don't moral and prudential problems come with knowledge of these psychological tendencies? The answer is yes. For instance, psychological knowledge improves persuasive power and, like other power, it can be used for good or ill. Captain Cook once played a psychology-based trick on his seamen to cause them to eat sauerkraut and avoid scurvy. In my opinion, this action was both ethical and wise under the circumstances, despite the deliberate manipulation involved. But ordinarily, when you try to use your knowledge of psychological tendencies in the artful manipulation of someone whose trust you need, you will be making both a moral and prudential error. The moral error is obvious. The prudential error comes because many intelligent people, targeted for conscious manipulation, are likely to figure out what you are trying to do and resent your action.

My final question is: Aren't there factual and reasoning errors in this talk? The answer is yes, almost surely yes. The final revision was made from memory over about fifty hours by a man eighty-one years old, who never took a course in psychology and has read none of it, except one book on developmental psychology, for nearly fifteen years. Even so, I think the totality of my talk will stand up very well, and I hope all my descendants and friends will carefully consider what I have said. I even hope that more psychology professors will join me in: (1) making heavy use of inversion; (2) driving for a complete description of the psychological system so that it works better as a checklist; and

(3) especially emphasizing effects from combinations of psychological tendencies.

Well that ends my talk. If in considering what I have said you had ten percent the fun I had saying it, you were lucky recipients.